A **PENNY TASSONI** HANDBOOK

GETTING IT
RIGHT FOR
TWO
YEAR
OLDS

HODDER
EDUCATION
AN HACHETTE UK COMPANY

The publisher would like to thank the following for permission to reproduce copyright material:

Photo credits: page 21: © Arkady Chubykin/Fotolia; page 27: © Sport Moments/ Fotolia; page 61: © Craig Holmes Premium/Alamy; page 90: © Howard Shooter/ Dorling Kindersley/Getty Images

Although every effort has been made to ensure that website addresses are correct at time of going to press, Hodder Education cannot be held responsible for the content of any website mentioned. It is sometimes possible to find a relocated web page by typing in the address of the home page for a website in the URL window of your browser.

Orders: please contact Bookpoint Ltd, 130 Milton Park, Abingdon, Oxon OX14 4SB. Telephone: (44) 01235 827720. Fax: (44) 01235 400454. Lines are open 9.00–17.00, Monday to Saturday, with a 24-hour message answering service. Visit our website at www.hoddereducation.co.uk

First published in 2014 by
Hodder Education
An Hachette UK Company
338 Euston Road
London NW1 3BH

Impression number	5 4 3 2
Year	2018 2017 2016 2015

Cover photo © Getty Images/iStockbyte/Thinkstock
Typeset in Caecilia LT Std-Light 10/13 by Datapage India (Pvt.) Ltd.
Printed in India
A catalogue record for this title is available from the British Library.
ISBN 978 1 471 80799 2

Contents

About the author

Penny Tassoni is a well-known education consultant, author and trainer who specialises in the whole spectrum of learning and play. Penny has written thirty books, many of which are bestsellers in the childcare sector. Penny is a sought after speaker both in the UK and internationally, where she has worked in Istanbul, China and Japan. She is also president for PACEY, the Professional Association for Childcare and Early Years (formerly the NCMA).

Acknowledgements

A thank you once more to the Tassoni Team – Jean Michel, Anne Marie and Marie-Lise who support all aspects of my work with children. I would also like to thank Stephen Halder, Sundus Pasha and Jane Adams at Hodder Education for supporting this project. My thanks also go to Julie Breading and the team at Ark Alpha Nursery, Portsmouth for their interest and support. I would also like to thank Kym Scott of Lewisham School Improvement Team for her useful comments and encouragement. Finally, I am grateful to Nicola Amies at Bright Horizons Family Solutions for inspiring me to write this book.

The publishers would like to thank all the staff, children and families at Vanessa Nursery School, Godinton Day Nursery, Ark Alpha Nursery, and Bright Horizons Family Solutions for their help with many of the photographs, taken by Jules Selmes. A special thanks to Michele Barrett, Jenni Hare, Julie Breading, and Susan Goodbrand for all their assistance with the organisation of the photoshoots.

Foreword

Two year olds are unique and deserve respectful understanding of their special stage of development. All of us were two once: some of us have vivid memories of the joy of exploring the properties of snow, mastering the complexity of skills to get into a go-cart and propel it forward with our feet, or the sheer pleasure of sharing a much-loved book with a significant carer in our life. However, how many of us also recall the overwhelming frustration of an adult, a well-intentioned one, just not appreciating that watching a snail slithering along was far more important than getting to the bus stop on time, or just how annoying that nice caring adult could be when they insist that you keep everything tidy! Being two is probably the most explosive period of development on a child's journey through childhood so it rightly deserves a whole book dedicated to celebrating and understanding the uniqueness of being two.

Penny Tassoni is not only passionate about child development, play and learning she is also immensely knowledgeable and a well-seasoned advocate for children. This latest book provides the 'Tassoni style' of wise, pragmatic, down-to-earth guidance on everything an early years educator needs to help them navigate the rewarding, and at times complex and puzzling, world of caring for and guiding the play and learning of two year olds. Packed full of underpinning knowledge, tips and ideas for fun learning activities, and importantly, guidance on talking with and supporting parents, Penny helps early years educators get to know and understand two year olds in ways that will soften the heart of their most reluctant fans. For some two year olds may be noisy and chaotic learners, for the initiated they are busy discoverers and investigators embracing the world they have set out to explore with the support of warm, loving, secure relationships with their significant carers.

Nicola Amies

Director of Early Years

Bright Horizons Family Solutions.

How to use this book

Whether you are a student or a setting expanding its two year old intake, this book contains informative, fun and above all practical advice on how to best work with two year olds! The book guides you through developmental patterns, how to carry out the two year old progress check, how to create optimal environments and includes an array of activities. It is is divided into three parts:

Part 1 Getting to know two year olds

Part 2 The practicalities

Part 3 Adult-guided activities

Key features

Getting it right

- Apart from meal times, do not expect children to sit still for long periods.
- Based on observation of children, consider whether chairs are needed for play opportunities such as dough.
- Put out activities on the floor or on low tables that will allow children to squat.

The 'Getting it right' boxes comprise of checklists of best practice, tips and guidance on how you can ensure you get it right for two year olds.

Is there a best place for settling in?

Two year olds who are unsure often feel more relaxed in larger spaces, especially outdoors where they feel less trapped. If the weather is good, consider following the steps outdoors.

The 'Questions and concerns' speech bubbles address common concerns and questions faced by practitioners with helpful answers and advice.

Observation point

Look to see with which aspects of self-care a child is struggling. Work out whether the issue is linked to their technique or hand–eye coordination.

'Observation point' boxes provide guidance on specific things to observe and look out for when working with two year olds, and how best to incorporate observation as part of practice.

Adult-guided activities

Thirty practical activities for adults and two year olds to do together.

Introduction to the activity outlining instructions and safety points

Shows how the activity links to the prime areas of the EYFS with useful prompts and questions to assess the areas and ways to vary the activities

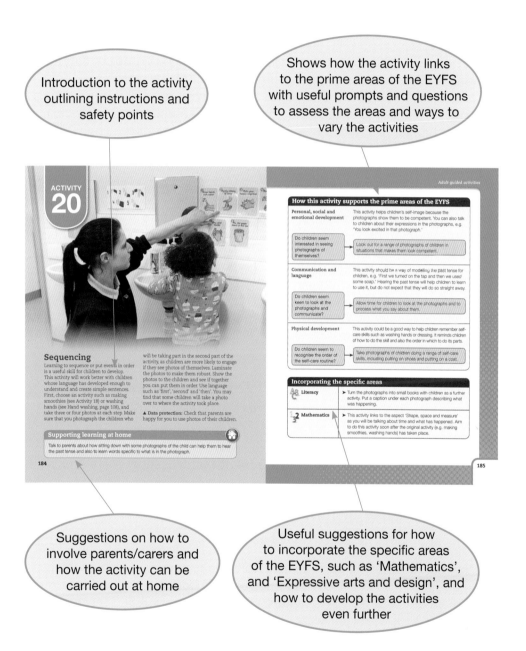

Suggestions on how to involve parents/carers and how the activity can be carried out at home

Useful suggestions for how to incorporate the specific areas of the EYFS, such as 'Mathematics', and 'Expressive arts and design', and how to develop the activities even further

Introduction

Welcome to my latest practical handbook! This book focuses on how to understand and best meet the needs of two year olds.

Two year olds are undoubtedly a very special group. While all groups of children are interesting, I think that there is something particularly extraordinary about two year olds. Their development can be spectacular with most children moving from two-word utterances to speech that is in simple sentences and fairly clear. Their play also changes dramatically with children becoming increasingly sociable and imaginative. This development though is not automatic. It is more likely to occur when they are being supported by knowledgeable, nurturing adults. This is of course why recent policy decisions have focused on providing funded places for children in this age group who come from families who may be experiencing some disadvantage. While the decision to fund two year olds in in early years setting may seem straightforward on paper, the reality is that great thought and care is needed if two year olds are to flourish in our settings. Contrary to the views of some policy makers, they are not just shorter versions of three year olds! They think differently, play differently and this is what makes them so special.

In this book, I hope to provide you with a very practical guide that will give you both knowledge and ideas about how best to work with two year olds. The book is divided into three parts:

Part 1 Getting to know two year olds
This section focuses on the development of this age range.

Part 2 The practicalities
This section looks at how to create an environment that will support children's development and also their play needs.

Part 3 Adult-guided activities
This section looks at ideas for adult-guided activities.

Finally, I know that a variety of early years settings take in two year olds, which includes child minders, so I have tried to reflect this in both my suggestions for the play environment and also for the activities. I hope that you will find this book useful and wish you good luck with your work.

Penny T.

PART 1

Getting to know two year olds

One of the things that I love about working with children, and especially with two year olds, is watching them grow and develop. In terms of working with this age group, understanding and recognising their development can make a huge difference.

In Part 1 we consider typical patterns of two year olds' development, including tips about how to observe them. For those of you working with the English early years framework, the Early Years Foundation Stage (EYFS), we also consider the two year old progress check.

A. **Features and patterns of development**
B. **Personal, social and emotional development**
C. **Communication and language**
D. **Physical development**
E. **The two year old progress check**

A. Features and patterns of development

If you know what is typical for the age and stage of an individual child's development, it becomes easier to plan activities for, create routines for and respond to them. Two year olds' development also influences how they play. Sustained role play, for example, usually only occurs once children are able to talk well.

The development debate

As with many aspects of early years education, opinion is divided about whether we should assess individual children's development in relation to that expected of the age group.

The argument against assessing an individual child's development against that of their age group is that children are not robots whose development will rigidly stick to a timetable; children are unique and measuring their progress against the traditional milestones of development is not helpful since it fails to recognise that rates of normal development vary. For several years, the EYFS has reflected this position. It was the reason why the age bands for achieving milestones given in the 'Development Matters' non-statutory guidance goals were so wide, e.g. 30–50 months.

Things are on the move again now in England. The direction of travel is towards trying to ensure that children who may need additional support are picked up at an earlier stage. There has been a call for more precise assessment, although the latest non-statutory guidance, published by the Department for Education and called 'Early years outcomes', still retains wide age-range bandings. The need to identify children who may need additional help is of course why in England the two year old progress check has been introduced (see The two year old progress check, page 60).

From my own perspective, I sit firmly in the middle of the debate about whether we should assess individual children's development in relation to that expected of the age group. I can see and have respect for both

Everyone agrees that assessment is important but there is debate about how it should look

sides of the argument. Children are unique and special and it would be a shame if we went back to a health model of child development whereby children's development becomes a series of checklists. On the other hand, I do see the traditional milestones as being rather like skeletons, in that they act as a framework for development. We all share the same bone structures apart from the odd rib, yet we can be different heights and have different features.

In the same way that doctors come to expect that certain bones will be in certain places, it is helpful to know what most children of a certain age will be doing. This is particularly important given that our education system is so rigid and no allowances are made for children's stage of development in teaching or testing. The statistics are bleak. Children who are not talking well when they enter school are not likely to master reading and so fall behind quickly. In this education climate, there is surely a duty to children to check that their development is close to the typical framework of development that most children share and to be ready to recognise if a child appears to be 'missing a bone'. The best way is probably to manage the assessment without becoming fanatical.

Tips for observing and assessing children's development

A good starting point for observing and assessing children's development is to be very clear about what it is that we want to achieve. While observation and assessment can help us reflect on our own practice and be fascinating in and of itself, observation has become something of a hot topic for many practitioners, who often feel that they have become paperwork-bound. The good news for settings in England is that there is a clear directive to keep observation and assessment to a minimum. I believe that there are five aims that we should be meeting when we observe and assess children shown below.

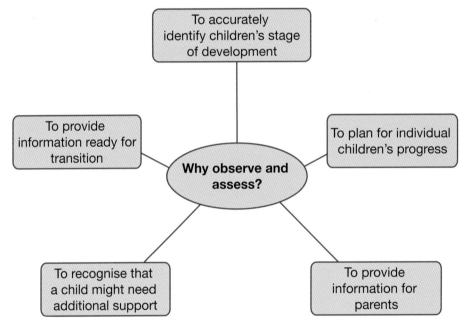

Why observe and assess?

What is needed?

If you agree with the five key aims in the figure above, the next step is to look at your current system. Of course, you may take a different view as to the purpose of assessment, in which case you should make sure that your system reflects your personal pedagogy.

Following are five questions that you might like to consider, which link to the five stated aims in the diagram.

1 Are you accurately identifying each child's stage of development? If so, how?
2 Are you using the information gained for planning? If so, how?
3 Do parents get the information they need and want? If so, how?
4 Is the information sufficiently accurate to pinpoint if children need additional support?
5 Are you providing the information that other settings need to help them with children's transition? If so, how?

How often should we observe?

This is often a great bone of contention in settings, with some practitioners feeling that they have to do one written observation every day. In terms of the EYFS, there is a clear direction that you need to record only that which is significant and/or will help you plan for the child's development. As most children's development does not change day on day, it is unnecessary to spend time writing up things that do not provide any additional information about the child's development. Of course, 'breakthrough' moments should always be recorded, such as a child managing to put their coat on without aid, but writing for the sake of it should be avoided.

Constantly observing

In the debate about observation, people sometimes forget that we should be constantly observing and noticing what children are doing. As a result of ongoing observations, most practitioners instinctively adapt their practice or the provision virtually minute by minute by putting out new resources or engaging a child further. It is all part of the job! The question is whether what we are seeing is sufficiently important that it needs writing down.

Observing while working with children

Most aspects of children's development can be observed while we are directly working with them, so the idea of a staff member taking half a day to observe children is usually unnecessary. Again, the EYFS is very clear about this and Ofsted will look to see how adults are using their time with children. They would argue that there is little point in spending half an hour staring at a child who we already know has a language delay when this time could be spent giving the child one-to-one interaction, and making notes either at the time or afterwards.

Right methods for right situations

When it comes to ways of observing children, there are plenty of different methods from which to choose. Practitioners will need to work out what they need to observe. Using milestones for the age group is helpful, not as a checklist but to know what to look out for, e.g. is the child showing hand preference? Can the child manage stairs?

What is Ofsted looking for?

Contrary to popular belief, Ofsted has no set views on what type of assessment methods are used. Ofsted is only interested in seeing whether you are able to identify children's stage of development accurately and whether you are planning in ways that will progress their development. To gain an outstanding, you will need to show that your assessment is 'precise' and also that you are working to ensure children who have come into the setting with development below that which is expected are rapidly making progress.

Once you know what you should be observing, it is then a question of using the most efficient method. Using a recording device such as an MP3 player, for example, is a far more effective way to record children's speech than using paper and pen. It has many advantages, not least that you can use it while interacting with children. You can also keep the recordings and play them again after a few weeks to assess whether individual children have made progress. Recordings are also liked by parents. In the same way, a well-timed three-minute video clip of a child using a piece of equipment or engaged in an activity is likely to generate plenty of information about their physical development – and again is liked by parents. Revisiting the situation with another later video clip will be a good way to check progress. Please note, however, that you must have written permission from parents for videos or any photos taken by practitioners/child minders, etc.

We have been told that we should be using learning journeys.

There is no statutory requirement to do so. While some settings use the learning journey approach, others choose not to. Think about what you feel is the best approach to record children's progress and also make plans.

Assessment – bringing it all together

While the paperwork of observation should be kept to a minimum, you do need to spend time doing some summative assessment. This means bringing together what you have observed about the child. This is where time and effort should be spent as assessment is key to effective planning and also to recognising whether a child needs additional support. My advice to settings is that they do a short summative assessment on each two year old every four to six weeks.

The focus for assessment should be on the prime areas for two year olds (personal, social and emotional development; communication and language; physical development), with some additional comments about other areas of development. Look back at significant written observations and recordings. It is good practice to talk to parents about what they have seen their two year old do at home. Use all the available information to work out what progress has been made. All summative assessments should be dated so that you can track an individual child's progress.

Once you have considered the children's progress, think about what type of activities and resources might benefit the child further. These are the 'next steps' in terms of planning for the child's future development. These should then feed into your short-term planning, e.g. what you do on a day-to-day basis.

Starting point

The first summative assessment should be done very soon after a child comes into your setting. This first assessment will be the child's starting point in terms of later review of their progress. It should look at the prime areas and be based on what you have been told by parents as well as what you have observed so far. You may not get a full picture of what a child is able to do, but you can follow up the 'starting point' assessment with another summative assessment after a few weeks.

Some practitioners say that they cannot write a summative assessment without spending several weeks with a child, but I disagree. As professionals, we should be able to work out after spending a week with a child whether he or she is moving well, has reasonable hand–eye coordination and whether or not the child has some speech!
After all, other professionals, such as speech and language therapists and paediatricians, often have just half an hour in which to make an assessment.

It is important to recognise children's development when they first start at your setting

Talking with parents about their child's progress

It is sensible to talk with parents about their child's progress in the run-up to completing a summative assessment. You may, for example, share with parents that you are on the 'look-out' for a certain skill and ask them to let you know if they see it at home.

There are many advantages to this approach. Not only can parents tell you about what their child is doing at home, it also means that if the child is not showing expected development in a particular area, that they will not be surprised to hear about it. While we need to reassure parents that children

Getting it right

- Avoid waiting a period of time before letting parents know that you have concerns about development.

do not follow a neat schedule when it comes to development, parents do have the right to know if you suspect there is a delay. Sometimes it may be that you agree to both keep an eye on this area of development over the next weeks, or you may agree that a referral would be wise, especially if you know that waiting lists are high in your area.

Who should tell a parent that their child might have a delay?

Ideally, this should be the child's key person, provided they have the experience and knowledge to do so.

How should you start a conversation with parents if a child is thought to have a delay?

Ideally, you should have already let parents know that you are observing their child as a matter of routine. Start by asking parents how they feel about their child's development. It may be that they are already aware that their child might need additional help, or equally they may mention factors that are currently affecting their child and thus their development. Throughout any conversation with parents, think about what it might like to be in their shoes. Most parents want to feel that their child is 'special' and 'liked' and so do not make 'concerns' the only focus of your conversation.

What happens if we agree that there may be a concern?

Talk with the parents about what they might like to do after suggesting the possible options. These will depend on the level of concern but might include monitoring further, drawing up a plan to support the area of development at home and also in the setting, or agreeing with parents that referral to other professionals might be useful. Before talking with parents, do make sure that you know how referrals can be sought in your area. In some areas, parents will need to contact their health visitor, while in others there may be a direct referral system.

Patterns of development

Over the next few pages, we will look at the typical patterns of development associated with children aged from eighteen months to three years, as it is worth knowing that not all children will neatly fit into the two-to-three-years development range. These typical patterns of development are based on the classic milestones originally written by Mary Sheridan in *From Birth to Five Years* and on materials from the I CAN charity, as well as a range of other sources.

While I hope that these will be useful, please remember that they are only a guide. If you look at any reference book, you will probably see that there is a variance between the different milestones, especially when it comes to speech. To help you work out whether you should seek help for a particular child, look out for the questions and answers speech bubbles. As individual children's development closely affects our practice, look out also for the 'Getting it right' boxes and 'tick' icon.

B. Personal, social and emotional development

Personal, social and emotional development is a prime area within the EYFS. It is a good starting point when looking at children's development. There are three aspects that form the early learning goals: making relationships, self-confidence and self-awareness, and managing feelings and behaviour.

Making relationships

The starting point when looking at making relationships is attachment. It is important for anyone working with young children, especially two year olds, to know this age group's attachment needs and behaviours. Understanding attachment will help you to support children with settling in and work more effectively with parents. It will also help you to make sure that your processes are seen as effective when inspected. This is important because Ofsted now checks whether children's attachment needs are being met.

Attachments are the close relationships that tie adults and children together. The first and usually strongest attachments that are made are between babies and their parents. These attachments are thought to be of great importance as they offer the growing child long-term emotional security and also physical security. Parents will go to extraordinary lengths to protect and nurture their offspring and this seems to have been programmed into us by evolution. It is this programming that usually makes it hard for parents to leave their children when they first come into a setting (see also Settling in, page 82).

As well as making attachments to parents, babies and young children can also make attachments to other people, such as other family members, and this means that many children have a network of people that they can trust. These attachments are not usually as intense as those that the child has with their parents and this means that in the event that a child needs reassurance and has a choice, they will turn to their parent first.

Effects of separation

Children who have strong attachments show a pattern of distress when they find themselves without anyone with whom they have an attachment. This distress is known as 'separation anxiety' and is thought to produce long-term effects on children's development. At first, children usually shout, scream and cry loudly. This is called 'protest'. It is a way of signalling to the parent or other attachment that they need help. The key features of protest are its loudness, distress and persistence. This is not a few quiet tears that quickly pass!

The next phase of separation anxiety is the opposite: silence. Children become quiet, withdrawn and very passive. Unfortunately, some adults think that this means that the child is fine and has accepted their lot. They are wrong. In this phase children are in a depressive state, which is harmful for their overall well-being and future ability to cope with changes and transitions.

Interestingly, parents too show behaviours linked to separation anxiety. I crudely categorise these behaviours into either 'long lingerers', who struggle to leave, or 'cut and runners', who cope by trying to get the separation over with as quickly as possible. Parents who have experienced leaving their children upset report high levels of stress and anxiety. This is probably a deliberate ruse by nature to ensure that parents stay and protect their offspring.

The good news is that separation anxiety, for both children and their parents, can be avoided. This is the basis of the key person system, which is now mandatory for all EYFS settings. A key person is in effect an additional attachment for the child. In Part 2 we will look at the nuts and bolts of how to support children as they settle in and create this additional attachment.

Attachment behaviours

As part of children's need to have strong attachments, there are some behaviours that are common among this age group, especially children's need for proximity to their parents or main carers and their wariness of strangers. It is important to recognise these as being developmentally typical rather than problematic.

Proximity

A key feature of this age group's attachment behaviour is their need to be physically close to or at least in sight of an adult with whom they have an attachment. The need to be constantly close begins soon after children reach their first birthday, with toddlers protesting when their parent is out of sight. Many parents will report that even in their own home they cannot so much as go to the toilet without their two year old coming along, too!

Children will often want to be picked up or to sit on 'their' key person's lap, then only a minute later to want to get back down again.

It seems that frequent bursts of physical contact are needed in order for children to be reassured. This can be very wearing for adults, but it is important to recognise that it is a usual pattern of development. Many children will start to increase their 'range' and be able to play further away from 'their' adults as they reach their third birthday. They may, for example, happily play with other children for fifteen minutes without feeling the need to keep a check on where 'their' adult is.

Two year olds show proximal attachment behaviours

Wariness of strangers

Along with the proximal attachment behaviours, children at two are also likely to be extremely wary of unfamiliar adults approaching them. This, along with their need to stay close to their parents or other familiar adults, is thought by many to be an evolutionary device. It prevents young children who have no notion of safety from wandering off with potentially hostile strangers. Wariness of unfamiliar adults plays out in a variety of ways. Expect to see the most wary children hiding behind their parent's legs or breaking off from their play to be closer to them. Some children just stay close but stare out at a 'new' adult while steadfastly refusing to engage in any interaction. I suspect that the extent to which children show behaviours depends on a number of factors, including:

- the temperament of the child
- their level of curiosity
- how much experience they have had of being with others.

Children who have been in daycare since they were babies, for example, may be used to seeing a number of adults popping in and out, wariness of strangers is usually less pronounced in these children. Their parents will have dropped them off and collected them at different times, and they will also be used to changes in their key person when shifts start and end or for holiday cover. On the other hand, most young two year olds, who come into a pre-school for the first time and have never been out of sight of their parents or close family members, may exhibit more wariness.

Wariness of strangers decreases as children get older and so you are likely to see quite a difference in children as they reach their third birthday.

Observation point

Look at how children tend to seek out their parents or a familiar adult when they need reassurance or are unsure of a situation.

Getting it right

- Wariness of strangers will be a barrier for children who start in settings at two, so good settling-in procedures are essential (see Settling in without tears, page 82).
- If you work in a group care setting, such as in a pre-school or a nursery, there are some additional points to consider. Free flow play might not be that effective for some two year olds because of their proximal attachment needs. Consider observing whether the two year olds are simply moving from one adult to another rather than actually making play choices (see The role of the key person, page 76).

Factors affecting attachment

While most parents and children develop healthy models of attachment by which the child responds well to the parents and vice versa, there are some factors that can affect parents' ability to respond to their child appropriately (see the diagram below). The process of attachment usually involves parents spending time cuddling, smiling at and soothing their babies. This in turn usually elicits a positive response back from the child, i.e. the child may coo or stop crying, and this in turn encourages the parent further. A positive cycle of behaviours starts to appear and from this the baby learns to trust their parent, while the parent gains confidence and also pleasure from being with their child.

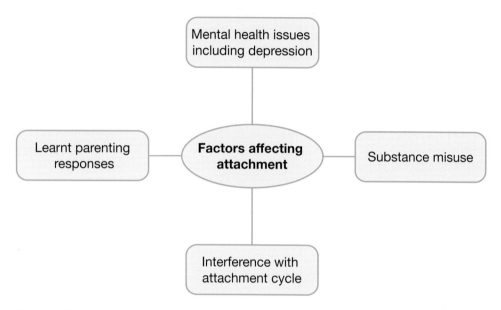

Factors affecting attachment

Mental health issues

Some parents may have mental health issues, which may prevent them from showing the usual attachment responses. In addition some medications may also alter the level of emotions that the parents can express and feel towards their child. Depression is a common cause of attachment difficulties. While there are many triggers for depression, many women after birth experience postnatal depression, which is caused by a hormonal imbalance. It is thought that at least fifteen per cent of mothers will experience this type of depression, although many will not seek help.

Substance misuse

Parents who have an addiction to drugs or alcohol are less likely to be emotionally available for their child. They may show very inconsistent patterns of behaviour depending on their mood and state of health.

Interference with the attachment cycle

For some parents, attachment difficulties occur because the attachment cycle cannot establish itself. The first few months seem to be critical in establishing this cycle and so anything that interferes with this can be problematic. It is common, for example, for there to be more attachment difficulties with premature and sick babies, as parents may not be able to cuddle and touch their children. The prematurity of the babies may also affect their ability to respond. They may not stare into their parents' eyes or stop crying when parents try to soothe them.

Some mothers also have difficult births involving quite a lot of medical intervention and, again, they may not be in the position to initiate the cycle.

Learnt parenting responses

Many people think that parenting should come naturally and that it is totally instinctive. It would appear that this is not quite the case. A key factor seems to be how well the parent was parented themselves. Parents who experienced harsh, inconsistent responses from their own parents are likely to replicate the same with their own children. Parents whose own childhood had many disruptions in terms of who took care of them are also likely to struggle with the attachment cycle. Happily, with timely intervention parents can learn to modify how they behave towards their babies and young children.

What are the signs that children are not attached to their parents?

If children do not have a sufficiently strong attachment to their parents, you may see a range of atypical behaviours. It is important to pick up on these, especially if a child has been referred by a health visitor or social worker. Keep an eye out for children's responses on their first visit when they are not yet familiar with you or the environment. These children may:

- seem to avoid contact with their parent and not use them as a 'safe base'
- seek out physical contact with you as opposed to going to their parent
- seem indifferent to any adult, including their parent.

If you do have concerns about how a child is responding, always seek advice and guidance as early intervention can be helpful for both parent and child. This is because, unfortunately, there is a link between attachment and abuse; do be vigilant and again if necessary pass on concerns promptly.

Getting it right

- Let parents know that their two year old is not 'shy' if they appear wary of strangers.
- Expect that children will take time to build a relationship with a key person.
- Develop strong settling-in procedures that protect children from separation anxiety.
- Observe over time the way that children start to become more independent.
- Be vigilant for signs that parents are not coping and signpost information for them.

Relationships with other children

Many parents hope that their children will quickly develop friendships. Unfortunately, children's social skills are very much in development and so it is rare to find the type of reciprocal, mutual care and cooperation that underpins what most people would consider to be the basis of a true friendship. So what can we expect of this age group?

Interest in and awareness of other children

By the time children reach two years, you would expect to find that they are interested in other children of their own age.

- At eighteen months, most children will spend some time looking to see what others are doing, although this might be just glancing across. At two years you can expect to see children engaged in the same play activity, exchanging the odd glance, but otherwise it is almost as if they are in their own bubble.
- At two and a half years, many children will fleetingly play with children of their age. Expect to see good eye contact and enjoyment during these moments. There may also be the odd exchanges of equipment, e.g. if a child is dropping things into a bucket another child may pass something across.
- At three years, most children are playing quite cooperatively for periods of time, often with just one other child. What seems to bind children together is their play interest, so if one child leaves an activity for another in which the other child is not interested, the other child may not follow.

Older children

When it comes to playing with older children, much depends on the age difference. In home-based settings where two year olds might be with five year olds, there may be quite a lot of play activity depending on how patient and interested the older child is. Tensions sometimes abound when two year olds try to join in with the play of slightly older children, who resent the two year old not doing as they are told or not understanding the purpose of the play.

Cooperative play can sometimes be seen when two year olds are with older children

Modelling

While children may not show cooperative behaviour until they are at least three, many children do show clear signs of enjoying being with others. One of the ways in which we can see this is that children will often copy one another's actions. This is known as modelling. A good example of this is the way that at meal times one child will start banging the table and then all the other children will join in!

The desire for children to copy the actions of another child will often lead to squabbles. The classic example of this is 'pushchair wars'. One child is happily playing with a toy pushchair. Another child sees the first child and wants to do the same. The trouble is that there is only one pushchair. A squabble ensues!

Getting it right

- Let parents know that it is unusual for two year olds to have cooperative friendships in case they have concerns that their child is lonely.
- Observe how much cooperation children are showing towards other children in their play, but do not base routines or layout around such cooperation.
- Recognise when modelling is taking place and note which children are quick to copy and join in, as this is a positive sign.
- Note if there are any children who never seem to copy the actions of others.
- If modelling occurs while children are playing, try discreetly to provide sufficient resources so that children can continue with it and avoid a tussle over resources.
- Never have just one pushchair!

What should I do if I see that a child does not play with other children?

While we know that most children do not play cooperatively with others until three, it is worth noting if a child has absolutely no interest in others. Keep an eye on the child and watch out for any other indicators that might suggest atypical development.

Self-confidence and self-awareness

While these are linked areas, I am going to look at them separately and I suggest that you do this too when writing any assessments.

Self-confidence

Anyone who has worked with children knows that some children are keen to try anything and seem to be very confident. Other children hang back and may need some encouragement before trying things out. Self-confidence is a tricky thing to nail down in children's early years and so it is difficult to put pegs in the ground as milestones. Self-confidence is very dependent on the quality of relationships children have with adults. This means that children in their own home with their parents can be very confident, but in settings may appear to be lacking in confidence. The environment also plays a part. Children who are familiar with the environment and who know what they can and can't do or touch are likely to seem confident. Inconsistent rules and expectations on the other hand may make some children appear less confident.

Another factor to consider when looking at self-confidence is how we as adults judge a child to be confident. We often look at confidence in terms of how keen children seem to try out new things and how they gain our attention. A child who is quieter may seem less confident, but in reality a child who always wants our attention may be the one who is more 'needy'. There are no milestones when it comes to confidence, but here are a few things to think about when focusing on individual children.

Observation point

- What do parents think about their child's confidence at home?
- How independent is the child?
- How much adult attention do they need and how do they seek it?
- How relaxed is the child in the setting? Look at body language, for example, smiles, movements.

Getting it right

We know that children's confidence comes from gaining positive responses from adults. It also comes when children have had plenty of opportunities to feel successful.

- Provide opportunities so that children can learn to make simple choices.
- Set up plenty of open-ended experiences where there is no right or wrong way to play, e.g. sand, gloop (a mixture of cornflour and water).
- Check that every day each child has opportunities for warm, positive interactions with their key person.
- Show children photographs in which they appear competent, e.g. doing a painting.

Self-awareness

Self-awareness covers many things, from children learning to recognise themselves in the mirror through to understanding what it means to be a girl or boy (gender concept).

- By eighteen months – Able to recognise themselves in the mirror and also point to a photo of themselves.
- At two years – Most children know whether they are a boy or a girl and can also point to a picture of a child who is of the same gender.
- At three years – Most children can recognise physical characteristics that might give a clue as to another child's gender, e.g. hair length, style of dress.

Interestingly, it takes a couple more years before most children work out that if a boy puts on a dress, he remains a boy.

Observation point

- Notice to what extent children are starting to develop gender concept.
- Watch for children starting to show feelings of embarrassment or shame.

By eighteen months, children can recognise themselves in a mirror

Getting it right

Self-awareness is a journey for children. They will constantly pick up cues as to who they are based on what they see and our responses to them, and also how they are doing compared to other children. To ensure children have a positive image of themselves:

- Make sure that there are no 'favourites' in groups of children.
- Provide positive acknowledgement of effort as well as achievement.
- Show children that you like them for themselves, not just because of what they do.
- In mixed-age groups, explain to younger children that when they are older, they will be able to achieve more.
- Notice children who are showing embarrassment or shame, and show the child that they are still loved and liked by you, e.g. with a hug.

Gender

While most two year olds are only starting to differentiate between genders, they will soon be working out what it means to be a boy or a girl. This usually comes as children get closer to three years and so is not so much of a problem with the younger two year olds. It is important to recognise when this starts to happen and also to explain to parents that, as part of normal development, children may want to explore a range of roles. The classic example of this is the boy who loves wearing frilly dresses and playing with dolls. Another reason to spot children who are clearly exploring gender roles is that sometimes this can lead to them cutting down on the range of play opportunities and activities with which they will engage.

Getting it right

- Provide plenty of play opportunities that are non-gender specific.
- Take photographs of children playing with toys or engaging in activities that challenge popular conceptions of what boys or girls are 'meant' to play with, e.g. a group of girls playing football or a group of boys around a writing table.
- Audit resources carefully to reduce the amount of 'pink' or 'blue' as these colours often signal to children that they can or cannot play with things.

Managing feelings and behaviour

It would be silly to suggest that working with this age group is not without its challenges. Behaviour is one of those hot topics that keeps coming up. While we will look at how to promote positive behaviour in Part 2 (see page 93), in this section I want to look at the developmental patterns that lie behind this age group's behaviour.

Impulsivity

A good starting point is to be aware that this age group is highly impulsive. 'I see, I want and I grab without thinking about the consequences' seems to be the motto of children, particularly those under two and a half years or those with minimal language. They are also fast and quick off the mark if there is something they want to do. Their motor skills and coordination are no longer holding them back! There are many reasons why children in this age group are so impulsive. Firstly, we have to understand that the part of the brain that deals with planning and organising, the frontal lobes, is only just starting to develop. This means that children are not likely to be able to think through the consequences of their actions. In some ways it is like having no internal braking system. They may push another child down the slide because they want a go *now*, or they may hit a book over an adult's head seemingly for no good reason. There is little point therefore in asking a young two year old why they did something because they are not likely to know themselves. It just happened.

Children's impulsivity and restlessness increases when they are tired and so having good sleep routines is essential.

Interestingly, in my experience, language seems to make a huge difference to children's impulsiveness. This means that by three years, when most children should be talking in sentences, they are far less impulsive, and two year olds with great language skills will also be less impulsive.

The implications of this impulsivity are significant. It means that keeping children safe has to be a priority. A child might have been told not to touch something or to stay still, but there is no guarantee if they see or want something that they will remember this. Understanding children's impulsivity is also a clue as to why children may find it hard to share, may have tantrums or may not follow instructions.

Activity

Many parents and some practitioners underestimate children's need for movement. 'They are always on the go!' is a common cry. The good news is that being active and restless is typical for children at two and also at two and a half years. This age range likes to be busy and this plays out in a number of ways, including children wanting to take things from one place and then back to another, and also explains the difficulty they have in sitting for meals (see Meal times on page 113 for how best to manage this) and other parts of the routine.

Observation point

Think about children who do not seem restless and active. There are many reasons why this might be, including delay in motor skills, lack of sleep or an underlying medical issue that may need to be flagged up.

In a period when there is great concern about children not having sufficient exercise, it is perhaps helpful that this age group already wants to move around such a lot! Interestingly, the minimum activity level for children under five years who are walking unaided is three hours a day according to the Start Active, Stay Active guidelines. These can be found on the Department of Health website, www.dh.gov.uk.

Two year olds are very active

Regulation of emotions

This is quite a complex area, but we do know that two year olds' ability to regulate their emotions is still developing. This means that a two year old can go from distraught end-of-the-world-disaster mode to sunny laughter in a space of a few minutes! In the same way that children's impulsivity seems to wane as they approach three, so we find that these huge fluctuations in children's moods start to calm down. This again seems to be linked to developments within the brain and the levels of language that children have, but also to how well the key people in children's lives respond to them. Inconsistency or unresponsiveness to children seems to prolong this stage.

As most people know if they work with this age group, tiredness makes an already emotionally labile child even worse, and so a good sleep routine is essential (see also Sleep on page 124).

A lot is said about 'teaching' children to control their emotions but, when it comes to two year olds, I fear that this might not be very useful. Acknowledging children's emotions seems to be helpful, though.

Observation point

Think about whether there is a pattern to children's moods and ability to cope. It may be that lack of sleep, hunger or another issue is making things worse.

Getting it right

- Keep a good pace with children as they do like to be busy.
- Avoid holding inquests into children's behaviour – they are unlikely to be helpful.
- Check whether children are sleeping sufficiently as naps can make a difference (this is covered in more detail in Sleep on page 124).

Tantrums

A feature of many two year olds' behaviour is tantrums. Tantrums link closely to children's high impulsivity and difficulties with emotional regulation. This means that a two year old who sees something but cannot have will become frustrated and unable to control their feelings. Tantrums are seen from eighteen months onwards and are likely to rapidly decline in frequency when children reach three years.

The extent and frequency of tantrums can vary according to individual children. This is because there are several factors that affect their frequency and intensity (see the following diagram).

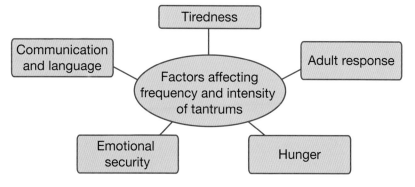

Factors affecting the frequency and intensity of tantrums

Communication and language

As we have seen, impulsivity and emotional regulation change as children develop, and this is linked to children's increased language skills. This means that two year olds who can communicate well are likely to have fewer tantrums. Their language skills allow them to understand simple explanations given by adults as well as responses such as 'You can have it after tea.' They are also more able to communicate their wishes and their frustrations using language.

Tiredness

When children are tired there is a higher likelihood that tantrums will occur, even if they have good language skills. This is because tiredness affects their emotional regulation.

Observation point

Work with parents to monitor the frequency and intensity of tantrums and to see if sleep is an underlying factor.

Hunger and diet

Many adults working with children and parents find that there are more tantrums just before meal times. This is likely to be linked to lower levels of blood glucose, which in turn affects children's ability to regulate their emotions.

A sugary diet can also impact on the frequency of tantrums. This is because sugar quickly raises the blood glucose in the body, but then falls away quickly, leaving the brain in the same state as when the body is hungry.

Getting it right

- Be ready to change the snack and meal times in your setting if you find that there is a correlation between tantrums and hunger.
- Check whether children are having sufficient opportunity to nap when they need to.
- Make sure that parents understand that sleep and a balanced diet will help to reduce the incidences of tantrums.
- It is also worth understanding that age-related impulsiveness will mean that children of this age will find it hard to see something but not be able to have it. It is therefore worth planning ahead and removing things that will cause frustration to children.

Adult response

How adults respond to tantrums can affect their frequency and intensity. Some children who begin by having typical age-/stage-related tantrums can go on to learn a tantrum response. This tantrum response is used whenever their wishes cannot be met and endures even once they have good communication skills. The usual reason why children develop an automatic tantrum response is that they have learnt that a tantrum somehow gets results – the adult may change their mind or 'give in'. It is important here to understand that children do not plan 'tantrums' as such – it is simply a learnt response, like a two year old learning that if they bang a spoon on the table, an adult is likely to turn around.

Interestingly, it can take a while for a child to unlearn a learnt tantrum response. While it is being unlearned, total consistency of adult responses is needed. This requires all adults to agree a response and to recognise that it may take a couple of weeks before the child's response changes. In this period, the length and intensity of the tantrum may even increase at first.

Observation point

Work with parents to consider what the usual adult responses are when a child has a tantrum.

Adults have to stay calm when a child has a tantrum

Emotional security

Tantrums seem to be more frequent where there are disruptions to a child's routine or changes in their lives. Children seem to need some level of consistency in order to feel safe. Tantrums can therefore be linked to stress. In addition, children are likely to have disrupted sleep patterns when there are changes to their routines, which can also exacerbate the situation.

Dealing with a tantrum

There is more than one school of thought as to what should happen if a child has a tantrum. Whatever approach you decide to take, the key is to remain calm and also to work with parents to develop consistent responses.

My preferred approach when dealing with an age-/stage-related tantrum is as follows:

1 Try to distract the child at the first sign of a potential tantrum.
2 If this fails, stay calm and be very quiet – allowing the child to go through the stages of the tantrum. Reassure any other children that all is well.
3 After the tantrum has finished, or while it is in its final stages, do something that might distract the child and move the situation on, e.g. get out a puppet or start reading a story book.
4 Physically reassure the child, if this is needed. Carry on the rest of the session as if nothing has happened.

Never tease or laugh at a child who is having a tantrum.

Dealing with a learnt-response tantrum

Dealing with tantrums that have become a learnt response is more testing. This is because they are often louder and can be more persistent. It is crucial to agree with parents a consistent approach, as inconsistency can increase the frequency and also the duration of subsequent tantrums.

1 Acknowledge the child's anger or disappointment, e.g. 'I know that you wanted it, but it is not possible this time. It is hard for you.'
2 Try then to distract the child, but do not give in.
3 Once the tantrum is underway, do not make eye contact or talk to the child – as this is hard, look at a magazine or turn your back on the child.
4 If the child hits you or tries in other ways to demand your attention, e.g. throwing things, simply say 'I can only help you when you are quiet.' Repeat this only once or twice.

5 Wait until the child has finished the tantrum before saying anything or making eye contact.

6 Carry on with the session as if nothing has happened, but freely offer physical reassurance if the child wants it.

7 Look for frequent opportunities to praise the child during the rest of the session.

Sharing and showing concern

Sharing

One of the statements that I love in Mary Sheridan's *From Birth to Five Years* relating to two year olds is 'Defends own possessions with determination.' Even at two and a half years, the milestone is that children have little concept of the need to share. This plays out in a variety of ways. The first child sitting at a dough table is likely to take all the dough and then find it hard to give any to the children coming afterwards. It also means that children may try forcibly to remove toys that they want to play with from another child. Being able to share is a skill associated with three year olds.

Having said this, two-and-a-half-year-old children can often manage what I would call 'structured sharing', whereby an adult might direct them to pass a piece of fruit to another child, which they will do providing that they know that there is one for them too.

Getting it right

- Recognise that tussles and squabbles are all part of life with a two year old and reassure parents if necessary.
- Do not punish or overreact, but distract the child and if necessary return items to their rightful owner.
- Give small quantities of dough or other such materials to each child to avoid children thinking that it is all for them.
- Look out for opportunities to practise 'structured sharing'.
- Comment favourably when you see children who are sharing.

Showing concern

While the concept of ownership might not be there, children even at two should begin showing some empathy towards others. This may not be long-lived, but do expect to see a child passing a toy or giving a clumsy hug to another child who is upset, particularly a child who is younger.

Getting it right

- Showing concern for others is linked to children's own experiences of being nurtured, and so this needs to be modelled for them even if it is just with a cuddly toy.
- Remember to praise and acknowledge children for their concern.
- Expect that children's concern for others may be very short-lived.

Biting

Biting is one of those age-/stage-related behaviours with which it is difficult to deal. It is particularly common between the ages of eighteen months and two and a half years. The causes of biting are similar to those of tantrums, i.e. impulsivity, frustration and limited language.

While tantrums affect mainly the child, biting is different as it means that another child may be injured. To make matters worse, some biters seem to favour a particular child and, while most reasonable parents will accept that their child has been bitten once, they are likely to become very cross if it happens again.

Situations when biting may occur

It is hard to pin down a reason behind a bite, as children do not plan them, but there are three situations when a bite is more likely:

1 When children are tired or hungry.
   This is because being tired or hungry affects their emotional regulation making them more likely to do something impulsive.
2 When a child wants something or is frustrated by another child.
   This is linked to two year olds modelling and also their difficulty with sharing (see previous pages). A bite might occur when a child wants an object back from another child or has seen something of great interest.
3 When a child is not engaged in play or with an adult.

Understanding why bites are often in clusters

Few children bite only once. The usual pattern is that once children have bitten, they are likely to bite again. No amount of telling a child that it is not a nice thing to do will prevent this. It is worth understanding a few points about the 'power' of a bite and why simply hoping that the child will not bite again is likely to be futile.

Learnt response

As with most of this age group's behaviour, biting can quickly become a learnt response. This means that if a child who has already bitten finds herself in the same situation and especially near the same child again, there is a high likelihood of another bite.

Sensory feedback

It is easy to forget that Mother Nature intended for us to find biting a pleasurable activity – hence the popularity of chewing gum! When children bite, they are getting a strong, immediate and pleasurable sensation. Biting another child's arm must feel like biting into a soft doughy bun. The sensory feedback from a bite is very powerful and it is this that means that once a child has bitten, another bite is likely. It is similar to the way that once you have tasted a chocolate, you are likely to reach out for another.

Adult attention

While the sensory feedback from a bite is often what makes the next bite very likely, some children go on to learn that they can get adult attention from biting as well. It is therefore important that you cut down on adult attention when biting incidents occur. It is worth remembering that adult attention, including eye contact and words, is still adult attention even if you are reprimanding the child.

Dealing with a bite

There is often no rhyme nor reason as to why a bite has occurred. Adults are often surprised at how quickly a bite occurs and how mostly they did not see that a bite was coming. This is one reason why bites are notoriously difficult to manage. So what should you do if a child has bitten?

1 Go straight over to the scene, but do not look at the child who has bitten – focus your attention on the victim. This is important because we do not want the biting child to learn that biting results in immediate adult attention as this may reinforce the behaviour.
2 Reassure the child who was bitten and if possible turn your back on the biter. All your attention should go to the victim. We also need to recognise that a child who has been bitten may become fearful of other children. (If you feel that the biter is likely to bite again while you are reassuring the child who was bitten, gently restrain them by holding their arm).
3 Once you have dealt with the child who was bitten, your focus now should be on preventing the next bite.

Should we get the biter to say sorry?

A more effective strategy is to ask the biter to find something that they can give to the child who was bitten to make her feel better. This might be a drawing or taking over a toy. This approach has many advantages as it is not only more meaningful but can also help the child who was bitten to feel less fearful of the biter. The danger of a child saying sorry is that it is often addressed to the adult not the victim. Adults also think that if a child says 'sorry' it will prevent another incident. In my experience of this age group, there is no link between saying sorry and a reduction of future bites.

Preventing the next bite

When it comes to biting, it is useful to be pessimistic. Like chocolate biscuits, one leads to another; this is because of the strong sensory aspect to biting that combines with other reinforcements to make it a powerful experience for the biter. To prevent another bite, you must start with the assumption that another is likely to happen in the next few hours or days. It is not a question of *if* the child will bite again but *when*. Your mission is to make sure that for a couple of weeks, the child is not put back in the situation where the bite occurred – otherwise it is like putting a piranha into a goldfish bowl!

With this in mind, it is worth taking the following steps.

Immediately following the bite

Following the bite, the aim is to get to the end of the session without another bite occurring.

1 Keep the child very busy and next to an adult at all times. The adult can interact with other children, but this child should always be next to them.
2 Keep the child's hands full – e.g. carrying things, using sensory materials.
3 Do not talk to the child about the bite, simply carry on as if nothing has happened.

The next session

Unless the child has been off for at least a week, take the same measures as above for two further sessions. It is important that a significant period of time occurs without a bite before you relax.

Observation point

If another bite occurs, it is worth thinking about whether there is a pattern. Note the place and the time the bites occur. You may find that bites occur only indoors, or just before lunch or nap time. This can help you work out at what times and in which places they are likely to occur in the future. The child must be engaged with an adult rather than left to play near other children at these times and in these places.

The following week

If you find after checking with parents that no further bites have occurred, you can start to allow the child to play without an adult next to them for *short* periods of time. These must be times when you are sure that the child is not likely to be hungry or, more importantly, tired. This play must take place in a totally different situation to where the child originally bit, e.g. if the bite took place indoors, the child plays outdoors. The child must be kept away from his victim during this period – this is to prevent a child from being bitten twice. The rest of the time, the child should be with an adult and be kept busy, although other children should be included.

The week after that

If you reach the next week without any bites occurring at home or in the setting, you can breathe a sigh of relief. Apart from the end of sessions or just before lunch, when the child is more likely to bite, the child can be reintegrated as before.

Talking to the parents of the child who has bitten

Many parents say that when their child has bitten another child, practitioners can sound very accusing. While we do need to let parents know what has happened, we must recognise that they are unable to remotely control their child from a distance and so it will always fall on us to prevent a bite. A useful starting point, therefore, when talking to parents of a child who has bitten is to reassure them that biting is very common. There is no research to show that children who bite at two years old go on to have a criminal career! Having said that, we do need to gain information from parents and share strategies to avoid another bite. It is always worth asking parents if their child has bitten them or another child or adult at home. Quite often parents say that this is not the case and I would be inclined to believe them as some children will only bite children of a similar age or will confine their bites to a particular setting.

While a parent cannot prevent a bite from happening when they are not there, it is worth exploring whether there have been some upheavals at home, and also the amount of sleep a child is getting and whether an earlier bedtime or a longer nap is needed. It is also worth thinking about increasing the amount of adult attention that the child has at home.

Some parents say that they will bite the child back. Does this work?

Ahhhh! Make sure that all parents know that it is illegal to bite a child, even your own. Parents need to know that if you heard that they had bitten their child that you would have a duty to report them as a safeguarding measure.

What should parents say to their child after a biting incident?

While parents do need to know about the bite, they do not need to talk about it to the child. We know that this age group is impulsive and that biting is an unplanned event. Getting a child to promise before a session that she will be 'good' will not actually make any difference to how the child behaves.

Talking to the parents of the bitten child

Ideally, as part of the admissions process, we need to make sure that parents realise that there are likely to be squabbles, tussles and the occasional battle scar when children of a similar age are together. Reminding parents of this conversation can be a starting point when having what can be a tricky conversation. While we cannot 'undo' the bite, we should be talking to parents about how we are going to prevent a further bite from happening and the steps we will take to keep their child safe. As some children are bitten by their 'friends', it is also worth agreeing with both sets of parents that their children should be kept apart for a week or so.

Getting it right

- Reassure parents that biting is simply an age-/stage-related behaviour.
- Recognise that following a bite, a child is likely to bite again unless a strategy is put in place.
- Remember that children do not deliberately plan to bite another child – the sensory feedback gained from the original bite is often the trigger.
- Keep a child who has bitten busy and never leave them alone with other children for at least a week.

C. Communication and language

'Communication and language' is the second prime area within the EYFS. As we have already seen, the ability of children to use and understand language seems to make a difference in terms of how they relate to other children, manage their emotions and also their impulsiveness. In theory, this should be an exciting time for children as they should be quickly picking up new words, enjoying rhymes and wanting to know what things are.

There is a correlation between the amount of quality time that children spend interacting with adults and how well they do. By and large, this can account for significant differences in how much language they have by the age of three. As children need to be fluent in their speech by four, checking that they are well on their way becomes very important and it is essential not to wait too long before seeking a referral for a child whose language seems delayed. Interestingly, Ofsted also recognises the importance of communication and language and it is a major focus for inspection.

Usual patterns of speech and language development

When looking for milestones of development, there is some variance between different sources, particularly when it comes to how many words children may be producing. I would not get too hung up on this, but instead would suggest that you focus on recognising those children who are not keeping up. In particular, you should keep an eye out for how well the summer-born children are doing, as if they become delayed by six or so months and this is not picked up, they may not be fluent on entry into reception. As the adult–child ratio on entry into reception is low, opportunities for extended interactions in pairs or alone are very limited and so they may well fall further behind.

Listening and attention

It is important to understand that two year olds' ability to listen and concentrate is very much in development. This is linked to the development of the brain as well as to their level of language. This has important implications when it comes to organising your routines, as circle times, when children are expected to listen to someone talking about something of no particular interest, are likely to be problematic (see also Two year olds alongside older children, page 67).

As with adults, children always listen better when what is being said is of interest to them. They also find listening easier when they are in some way involved with the task, e.g. they are more likely to follow an instruction when doing some cooking!

Observation point

Two to three years: Listens to talk when it is directed to them and is of interest to them, e.g. 'Charlie, do you like these?' Can listen to a short story with pictures, especially when in pairs or small groups.

Three to four years: Finds it hard to listen while doing something else at the same time, e.g. watching television and responding to a question. Can listen to a simple story with pictures in a group of six or so (providing it interests them).

Getting it right

- Recognise that children will find it hard to listen while they are busy doing something else – you may have to wait for a natural pause in their activity.
- Get down to children's level – kneel or squat so your eye contact is parallel with theirs.
- Use children's names first to signal that you are talking to them.
- Smile, as this helps children to focus their eyes on your face.

Understanding

Eighteen months to two years	Understands between 300 and 500 words.
Two years	Can follow simple instructions, such as 'Go find your coat.' Can point to body parts, such as head, nose and mouth. Can on request point to an object in a picture, e.g. 'Where's the…?'
Two and a half years	Can follow simple instructions with words such as 'under'. Can understand a simple story with pictures.
Three years	Can follow a two-part instruction, e.g. 'Get your coat from the cloakroom and bring it in here.'

Understanding of language

The understanding of language is important. Children have to understand the meaning of words as well as be able to produce them. One of the ways that we can see if children understand words is by noticing their responses. Children who know what a coat is will touch their coat even if they are not using the word yet. We can also check understanding by seeing how children use words in their speech and whether they fit the context.

Observation point

Some children who are learning English alongside another language may hear words and go on to use them, but may not understand their meaning. Use instructions, simple questions or games such as picture lotto to check that children understand the meanings of specific words.

Processing time

Adults often forget that there is likely to be a time lag between a child hearing words and understanding their meaning. This gap is because children's brains are busy processing the information. It is one reason why toddlers often wave goodbye well after their parent has left. The time lag between hearing the words 'bye bye' and realising that a movement has to be made is several seconds – by which time the person they are waving goodbye to has gone!

A feature of children's development is that over time processing speeds become quicker. A four year old is quicker than a two year old if they are both asked to name a familiar object, e.g. 'What's this?' – 'A banana.' Having said this, you may spot that two year olds are sometimes able to respond quickly to something you have said. This is because while overall processing speeds are slow, there is a range of factors at play (see below).

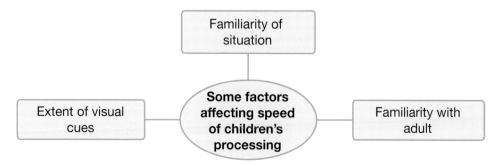

Some factors affecting the speed of children's processing

Familiarity of situation

Two year olds' processing times are likely to be faster when they are familiar with the context or situation. If a two year old is asked to get their coat every day, they are likely to respond fairly promptly. On the other hand, if children are asked to do something new, such as put out some beakers, they may be slower to respond.

Familiarity with an adult

Children who know us well are likely to respond more quickly, especially in a familiar situation. They recognise our body language and are also tuned in to our voices and expressions. This means that a new member of staff asking a child to do something that is otherwise part of the routine should expect a slightly slower response time.

Extent of visual cues

Children are always faster to process when there are visual cues. An adult who shows a favourite book to children and asks them whether they would like to hear it is likely to get a faster response than if they just name the title of the book.

Getting it right

- Remember that you must gain children's attention first.
- Keep your word count to a minimum and do not speak too quickly.
- Speak clearly.
- If asking questions or wanting children to comment, allow sufficient response time.
- Use body language and facial expression, e.g. point to things.
- Consider using visual props, such as pictures and puppets, to help children understand.
- Remember that with mixed-age groups, two year olds are always at a disadvantage when answering questions.

Speaking

While babies do babble and make sounds, the production of words comes after children have made the link between the sounds they are hearing and the meanings of words. Many of children's early words are either objects that they can see, such as 'dog', or simple actions, such as 'look' or 'go'. Children's early progress in speech is assessed at first by how many words they have. Counting words is therefore important. A word is a sound that a child makes and consistently uses for an object or action, even if it does not sound correct, e.g. 'dous' for juice or 'doddie' for dog.

When working out how many words children have, make sure that you talk to parents. This is because young children talk about what they are doing and seeing – it is very much in the 'here and now'. At home children will be doing and seeing other things. They are likely, for example, to have a word for 'bed' and for each of their family members.

Eighteen months to two years	Six to twenty words – some children will have more than this Points to objects of interest and uses a single word or vocalisation Enjoys nursery rhymes and may try to sing
Two years	Fifty words or more Puts two or more words together, e.g. 'Daddy car gone.' Uses own name when talking, e.g. 'Milly want that.' Asks names of objects and people and points to them Joins in nursery rhymes
Two and a half years	Two hundred words Uses simple sentences Knows full name Continually asks questions, such as 'What's this?' 'Who's this?' but not 'why' Is able to use 'I' and 'me' correctly instead of using their own name, e.g. 'I want that.' Can say a few nursery rhymes and responds to others
Three years	Large and continually growing vocabulary Asks continual questions, such as 'where', 'what' and 'who' Is able to carry out simple conversations and can talk about present and past events Knows several nursery rhymes Speech is sounding tuneful Speech can mostly be understood by an adult who does not know the child

Speaking (expressive language)

Children who speak another language at home

With children who are learning more than one language, total up the number of words across the languages. You will usually find that they will have more words in the language that they have spent the most time listening to and being interacted with. The advice for parents who want their children to be able to speak a home language as well as English is that they should keep using their home language. The danger otherwise is that over time, English will become so dominant that the child finds it hard to use the home language. It is also better for the development of English if children hear fluent speakers because they are less likely to make grammatical mistakes and will also allow children to hear the 'sounds' of English.

Features of two year olds' spoken language

Echolalia

It is normal for children at two years and still at two-and-a-half years to sound like parrots. This is called echolalia. You say something and they repeat it, sometimes several times. This tends to disappear at three years, but will of course depend on whether the child has age-related speech.

Self-directed talk

From eighteen months onwards children increasingly talk when they are alone and often as part of play. This type of talk is a healthy sign and should never be discouraged. It is a way for children to organise their thinking. Expect to hear quite a lot of this type of talk up until children are four or so. Even beyond four

Expect to see children talking to themselves while playing

years self-directed talk, although often done in private and quietly, remains important for problem solving, coaching and coping with stressful situations. So if you as an adult find yourself talking aloud, don't worry!

Observation point

Children like to talk into toy phones or mircrophones. This is a good time to listen to children's speech and if possible to record it.

Stammering/stuttering

Many children in this age group are likely to have moments when they hesitate during speech, causing them to repeat a word or sound several times. This is called stammering, and in most children is just a phase that will resolve itself without treatment. (Stuttering is similar but typically involves repeating a single letter rather than a whole word.) How adults handle this phase can make a difference, and there are some dos and don'ts when it comes to supporting children who are in a stammering stage.

Getting it right

- **Do** show the child that there is plenty of time and that you are in no hurry, e.g. sit rather than stand
- **Do** slow your own speech down slightly.
- **Don't** guess or finish off what the child is trying to say
- **Don't** set up competitive situations where children are able to call out and be the 'first' to say something
- **Don't** allow older children or more fluent children to interrupt your conversation with the child.

Observation point

When it comes to stammering, not all children need a referral but some do need additional support:

- Keep an eye on how frustrated a child becomes when speaking.
- Note how often a child is stammering and whether it is becoming a regular feature when the child talks.
- Find out from parents whether there is a family history of stammering.

Production of sounds

There will be many sounds that are unclear. This is because the mouth, teeth and tongue are still developing. The table on page 42 shows the sounds that you might expect to hear as well as the ones that children are not likely to be able to manage. It is worth knowing about these as sometimes parents become concerned, when their child is actually articulating correctly for their age. A good example of this is the way that most children will be saying 'dat' rather than 'that'.

Eighteen months	Makes the sounds p, m, b
Two years	Makes the sounds p, b, m, w Occaisonally difficult to understand what a child is trying to say unless there are visual prompts, e.g. a child pointing to an object
Two and a half years	Some words and phrases are becoming clearer, especially if the adult knows the child well Adults who are unfamiliar with the child are likely to find it hard to understand speech
Three years	Speech can be understood by people who do not know the child well Speech is tuneful and the child is very expressive
Refer if children are not producing	The sounds b, m, w
Speech immaturities are typical for these sounds	l, r, w, y, f, th, s, sh, ch, dz, j

Speech development in young children

Checking up on hearing

One of the major reasons why children fall behind with their speech or have problems with the production of sounds is because of hearing difficulties. A common cause of hearing difficulties is glue ear, which literally prevents the sounds of speech from being properly heard. It is very common in this age group. Unfortunately, unless you are actually looking for it, you may not pick it up. This is because the amount of sound that children with glue ear can hear varies. They may have some weeks when they are hearing quite well, but on other days they do not pick up so much. This can lead adults to think that a child is just not concentrating or is deliberately not paying attention. Just to make things a little trickier still, the amount of hearing can vary from ear to ear.

Observation point

It is important to look out for any sign of hearing impairment. Look out for children:

- whose reactions seem slower than other children's when instructions are being given, e.g. still sitting when others are starting to get up to get a snack
- who have little intonation or tunefulness in their voices
- who seem to stare at your face, particularly your lips
- whose parents report that their child turns up the volume on the television
- whose parents say that they have 'selective' hearing and only hear when they choose to.

Can a child who has 'passed' a hearing test still have a hearing problem?

Yes. Firstly, the tests that are done when children are babies are looking for a permanent hearing loss known as sensorineural. Children often develop conductive hearing loss, such as glue ear, later. Then, as stated above, we know that glue ear can be difficult to detect. A child may be booked in for a test when their hearing is good, but a few weeks later they may not be hearing as much. Many children have to be tested more than once.

D. Physical development

Physical development is the third prime area within the EYFS. Between the ages of two and three, children's movements and coordination flourishes. Physical development is important for children because it gives them more opportunities to learn. It also changes the way that children play with each other. There are significant variations in the physical development of different children. Some of these differences are linked to the opportunities that children have, others are likely to be linked to nature. Within the EYFS, there are two aspects within physical development: moving and handling, and health and self-care.

Moving and handling

This is the first aspect within the prime area of physical development. Moving and handling is a very broad area and covers children's ability both to make large movements and be mobile as well as their hand movements. It also considers children's general coordination. The development of children's handwriting skills is within this area of development as well. To help you assess children's development, we are looking at large movements (gross motor and locomotive movements) first, followed by the small hand movements that children also need to master.

Large movements – gross motor and locomotive

Being able to run, climb and balance seems to be important to children's overall development, as well as to their health and well-being. As we have seen earlier, children of this age group are usually very active. Being effortlessly mobile and also being able to climb allows children to see new things that they can learn and talk about. The view when standing upright is very different to that from the floor. Children's gross motor and locomotive development also links to how they play (see Recognising play patterns on page 132).

Observation point

Look at children as they are engaged in play. What posture seems to be the most comfortable for them?

Sitting

While it is usual to find small chairs in early years settings, many children between the ages of two and three actually prefer to squat or kneel when engaged in play. These positions seem to give children stability. They are also thought to be good for muscle development. As you may have already spotted, young two year olds often struggle to sit upright and still on chairs for any length of time. It is therefore important for snack times and other moments that chairs and tables are provided at the right height, as this can help children to be more stable. It is also worth noting that children are not likely to be able to sit cross-legged on the floor until they are at least three years old.

Getting it right

- Apart from meal times, do not expect children to sit still for long periods.
- Based on observation of children, consider whether chairs are needed for play opportunities such as dough.
- Put out activities on the floor or on low tables that will allow children to squat.

Walking and running

As you might expect, walking comes before running. With a few exceptions children are usually up and running by two years, although if children have global delay or were born prematurely, this might not be the case. Tackling steps, on the other hand, takes a little longer as balance is involved.

- At eighteen months – Walks with feet slightly apart (this creates the toddler gait). Holds on to adult to walk up and down stairs.
- At two years – Runs using whole foot. Can stop and start easily and manages to avoid obstacles. Can walk up and down stairs, but needs to hold on to a rail. Does not use alternate feet, i.e. one foot for each step. Instead, walks up and down stairs by putting first one foot and then the other on to each step.
- At two and a half years – Very confident walking up and down stairs but still holds on to rail and is likely still to not be using alternate feet.
- At three years – Walks up and down stairs using alternate feet. Can walk forwards and backwards. Can run and manage to avoid obstacles even when carrying something.

Coping with textures, slopes and dips

Children need to learn to walk and also run on different textures. They also need the opportunity to experience different types of surface, including slopes and dips. While at first children may slow down or even fall over, over time these types of surface will strengthen their movements.

Getting it right

- Create opportunities for children to walk on different surfaces.
- Audit your outdoor provision. Is there enough challenge for children?

Climbing

One of the characteristics of most two year olds is their enjoyment of climbing. It is almost as if they simply have to get their feet off the floor – even if this means standing on a brick! As with other aspects of physical development, there is a pattern to this.

- At eighteen months – Enjoys climbing up on to an adult-sized sofa or chair. Will climb forwards before turning around.
- At two years – Climbs on furniture and up a small slide.
- At two and a half years – Can climb carefully on a climbing frame.
- At three years – Can climb with confidence, e.g. on a climbing frame.

Observation point

Which equipment and areas do children seem to use for climbing? If these are not safe, how can they be removed or made safer?

Getting it right

- Audit your provision to source available indoor and outdoor climbing opportunities.
- Make sure that low furniture is sufficiently sturdy and stable to allow children to climb on to it.

Jumping

Being able to jump is a skill that requires balance and general coordination. There is also the matter of children's confidence. Most children do not attempt any sort of jumping until two years and it usually begins by a child dropping down from a low step, often while holding the hand of an adult.

Getting it right

- Allow children enough time to have a go at jumping.
- Offer a hand to start with so that children can experience the feeling of 'fall'.

- At two years – Drops down from a low step (no more than 30 cm), with one foot leading the way – almost like stepping.
- At two and a half years – As above, but able to tackle a slightly deeper step.
- At three years – Able to jump with two feet from a low step.

Most two year olds will need a hand when jumping from a high step

Kicking

Most two year olds are starting to be able to kick a stationary ball. At first they do this by merely walking into it. It will take them a while, however, before they can kick with any force. Football-crazy parents will have some time before their offspring is ready to play for a club!

- At two years – Kicks ball by walking into it.
- At two and a half years – Stands next to ball. Kicks ball gently, using whole leg. Knee not flexed.
- At three years – Stands next to ball, kicks ball with some force by bending knee.

Throwing and catching

When it comes to throwing and catching, there is a sequence of skills that children need to master. As you might have already noticed, children can throw before they can catch. This is because catching involves being able to accurately judge the movement of the ball. While practice can help children, it seems as if being able to judge time, distance and speed is also linked to brain development. Assessing children accurately is useful in terms of making sure that activities for them are not too difficult.

1	Overarm. No particular stance. Release is erratic and ball does not travel far. No accuracy.
2	Overarm (either arm). No particular distance. Release is erratic, but ball travels around one metre. Very limited accuracy.
3	Underarm (either arm). Tends to lean forwards with one leg advanced, deliberate release of ball increases. Some accuracy and distance.
4	Uses preferred hand. Leans forward, trunk moving with throw. One leg advanced, controlled release of ball. Fairly good accuracy and distance.
5	Movement is controlled, with the body arching back and then moving forward when throwing. Good stance and ball thrown with good timing. Ball travels far and accuracy is good.

Steps in learning to throw

In terms of what to expect from children between the ages of two and three, you are likely to see anything between stages 1 and 4. This is why careful assessment of individual children is needed. Children will need to feel successful in order for them to practise throwing.

1	Looks at the thrower, not the ball. Arms not ready. Little reaction apart from surprise when ball is thrown. No success in catching.
2	Looks at ball in thrower's hands. Arms out ready. Traps ball against chest. Fifty per cent success.
3	Looks at oncoming ball, but also at own hands. Arms ready and hands cupped in anticipation. Catches ball in hands most of the time.
4	Watches to see how ball is moving. Arms and hands move in anticipation. Catches direct throw easily and can even manage some throws to the side.
5	As stage 4, but movements are more coordinated and confident. Child is mostly successful even when they have to move to catch the ball.

Steps in learning to catch

As with throwing, there will be a huge variance in children's ability to catch, but most two-year-old children will be between stages 1 and 3. Children who are in stages 1 to 2 will need an adult to coach them and also for the ball/object thrown to be sufficiently large and malleable to make it easier to catch. They may also need the thrower to stand very close by.

Catching is a sophisticated skill that develops over time

Getting it right

- Provide objects that 'feel' good when children throw them, e.g. bean bags.
- Model throwing at easy targets, e.g. into a storage box.
- Recognise that catching is a developing skill – be patient!
- Provide soft large objects for children to practise catching.
- Do not expect that children can practise catching by throwing to each other – it needs an adult!

Fine motor development

As well as two-year-old children becoming increasingly coordinated, they are also developing the hand skills that are often referred to as fine motor movements. Most fine motor movements also involve the coordination of both hand and eyes, which is why activities such as threading are at first a challenge for children.

Hand–eye coordination

It is always worth noting children's hand–eye coordination and how they are doing in relation to expected development for their age. Delay may indicate that a child has additional needs, which can include the need for a pair of glasses! The traditional test of hand–eye coordination used by health visitors is to see whether children can place cubes on top of each other. This requires a lot of coordination and perceptual skills, e.g. understanding where the cubes are in relation to each other. Children will often need to see an adult build a tower first so that they get the idea.

Hand–eye coordination requires great concentration

- At eighteen months – Can build a tower of three cubes.
- At two years – Can build a tower of six cubes. Can turn over pages of a book, one by one.
- At two and a half years – Can build a tower of seven cubes.
- At three years – Can build a tower of nine or ten cubes. Can thread large beads using a lace.

Getting it right

Children need plenty of opportunities to practice and develop hand–eye coordination:

- Provide large beads for threading and also lacing cards.
- Encourage children to use cutlery at meal times.
- Give children opportunities to practise pouring, even if this is just in the sand and water tray.

Handedness

Between the ages of two and three years, children usually have developed a preference for using one hand rather than another. Hand preference is considered to be useful as it allows children to develop a pattern of how to approach tasks – using a stabilising hand and an active hand. Handedness is needed for many of the self-care tasks that allow children to become independent, such as dressing.

Very few children are ambidextrous, but if children do not have sufficient opportunities to use their hands they may be slow to develop a preferred hand. Interestingly, many household activities, such as peeling a banana and laying a table, involve using a stabilising hand and an active hand. Some speculate that insufficient involvement in such tasks at home may account for some children's slow development of hand preference.

Which is this child's stabilising hand?

- At eighteen months – Uses either hand.
- At two years – Starts to have a preferred hand that is used more frequently.
- At two and a half years – Preferred hand is observable.
- At three years – Preferred hand is established.

Observation point

To see if children have a hand preference, stand or sit directly in front of them and pass something to them. Make sure that you pass the object to the centre of their body, the mid-line. This is to prevent a child from just taking the object with the nearest hand. Do this at odd times and see if children start to be consistent. Also note how children use their hands during play.

Getting it right

- Provide plenty of opportunities for children to practise using one hand as a stabiliser while the other is active.
- Help parents to understand that they cannot influence which hand will be a child's preferred hand and interfering can cause later coordination difficulties.

Pencil grasp

This is quite a hot topic as pencil grasps in school-aged children are notoriously difficult to correct. The aim is that when children are around five they will have developed a dynamic tripod grasp. This grasp allows the pencil to make those bouncing movements that we use to make letters such as 'm' and also to join letters.

There are several stages that children will go through before they master a dynamic tripod grasp. Here are the three that you are likely to see with young children.

Palmar grasp

The palmar grasp is a whole-hand grasp that you might expect to see from eighteen months onwards.

This dynamic tripod grasp allows the fingers to flex

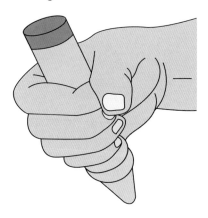

Palmar grasp

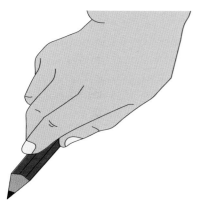

Digital pronate grasp

Static tripod grasp

Digital pronate grasp

Children using the digital pronate grasp will hold the pencil between two fingers and the thumb but in a very stiff way. Writing movements come from the elbow rather than from the wrist or fingers. This is the grasp that you are likely to see with most two year olds.

Static tripod grasp

Between three and four years children will start to use a static tripod grasp. The thumb is separated from the fingers. Movements come from the wrist rather than the fingers.

To support children through the pencil grasp stages, they will need plenty of opportunities to practise the movement used for threading or picking up something fine – the 'pincer grasp' movement. Children also need to develop general strength in their hands.

Getting it right

- Let parents know there is a sequence whereby children will develop the 'correct' grasp.
- Avoid correcting children unless you are sure they can use a tripod grasp.
- Make sure that there is a range of mark-making materials, not just pencils.
- Encourage large movements so that children's hands are not tense.
- Do not use tracing activities as this can prevent children from experimenting with new grasps.
- Look for activities that work on children's pincer movements, e.g. threading beads.
- Plan activities that involve strengthening movements in the hand, e.g. squeezing of sponges.

Observation point

- Watch to see how children are holding pens, pencils and other items such as brushes.
- See if children are developing from the palmar grasp.

Using scissors

Being able to use a pair of scissors requires a number of skills, including strength in hands, coordination of movements and also knowledge as to how to hold the scissors. Children also need to have acquired a hand preference so that one hand is stabilising the paper or material while the other hand is being active.

Not surprisingly, few younger two year olds (i.e. children who have just turned two, or are two and a few months) use scissors effectively. Many use a two-handed approach by which they try to cut as if the scissors were shears; others try to cut horizontally and have, of course, no joy. There is an argument to be made for waiting until children have developed a hand preference and strength in their hands. It may be comforting also for those of you under pressure to 'teach' children to use scissors to let you know that I have not found milestones that would indicate that children under three years would be skilful at using scissors.

Some children find it easier to stand than to sit when snipping

Getting it right

If you feel that a child has sufficient hand strength and coordination to manage scissors, you might like to start them on this ten-step teaching method, but do note that using scissors is difficult for this age range and so most two year olds will only be ready for steps 1 to 3.

1 Provide plenty of practice with tongs, then move on to tongs that open and close with a movement similar to that of a pair of scissors.
2 Give the child narrow strips of paper that require only one snip to cut, or put out some strips of dough for children to cut.
3 Draw lines across the strip of paper and see if the child can snip on the line.
4 Double the width of the strip of paper so that children have to open and close the scissors twice to cut across the strip.
5 Draw horizontal lines on the double-width strip of paper.
6 Use diagonal lines across the double-width strip of paper.
7 Encourage children to draw and cut along their own lines.
8 Draw curves on the strip of paper.
9 Start using wider pieces of paper and encourage the child to draw shapes on it.
10 See if the child can draw around a template of a circle and then cut it out.

Health and self-care

This is the second aspect within the prime area of physical development. For this age group, the focus in terms of development is what children can do for themselves, including toilet training. We will look in more detail at how best to support the toilet training process (page 118), as it is often a hot topic!

The link between hand–eye coordination and self-care

Many tasks, such as children being able to feed and dress themselves, are linked to how good their hand–eye coordination is. Proficiency at tasks is also linked to how much opportunity children have to practise them.

Self-care skills at different ages

I have pulled together a number of skills that children are likely to be able to do at different ages. Like all patterns of development, you should use this as a guide only. It is also worth noting that children often have quite a 'spiky' profile when it comes to self-care tasks as so much depends on the opportunities children have to acquire these.

Dressing

At eighteen months	Can take off shoes and socks.
At two years	Can put on a hat and shoes. Can also pull up trousers.
At two and a half years	Can put on a coat with assistance and can help with putting on a jumper. Can pull trousers up and down, but not able to put them on.
At three years	Can put on several items of clothing, but cannot manage fastenings such as buttons or zips. Will still need some assistance to dress.

Steps in learning to dress

Feeding

As with dressing, much depends on the opportunities that children have had in determining whether they are able to use cutlery. There has been a concern that children have too many finger foods and this is restricting their opportunities to learn. When talking to parents about feeding, it is worth recognising that cultures and individual families may have different approaches towards meal times and what is acceptable.

Two year olds need to be given cups not beakers as practice makes perfect

At eighteen months	Can use a spoon to eat with and most food gets in the mouth. Is likely still to be playing with food. Can lift a cup and replace it but may occasionally spill.
At two years	Uses a spoon well but is often distracted when eating. Can use a cup to drink from and can lift and place it down without spilling.
At two and a half years	Uses a spoon skilfully and may also now be using a fork.
At three years	Can use a fork and spoon.

Steps in learning to use cutlery

Variable willingness

You may have already spotted that two year olds can show variable willingness when it comes to self-care skills. There are a number of factors that might affect two year olds' willingness (see below).

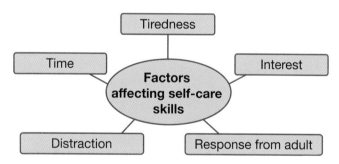

Factors affecting self-care skills

Tiredness

All bets are off when children are tired! Tiredness affects children's ability to concentrate and their coordination, so they may give up very easily or be reluctant to even try. Being ready to lend a hand or simply taking over is therefore sometimes the best option in these situations.

Interest

Some children are very keen to be independent and so are interested in mastering skills. They take great pride in showing off what they can do. Sometimes children with older siblings are keen to catch up with them, but then again sometimes the 'baby of the family' will let others do things for him/her.

Response from adults

How adults respond to children can make a huge difference to how keen they are to master skills. If adults overcorrect children or do not make self-care skills pleasurable, children are likely to respond badly. Equally, children can become frustrated if adults offer their help too early!

Observation point

Look to see with which aspects of self-care a child is struggling. Work out whether the issue is linked to their technique or hand–eye coordination.

Distraction

As we have seen, two year olds are impulsive and also find it hard to concentrate when there are distractions. This means that when something more interesting is going on, a child is less likely to be interested in eating or dressing.

Time

Self-care skills take two year olds quite a lot of time. There can also be some false starts, such as putting on a coat back to front or inside out. Not surprisingly, some parents find it easier to do the task for their children or create a rushed feeling. This tends to mean that children are less willing to try out their skills.

Getting it right

- Give parents a list of self-care skills that are age-/stage-appropriate for their child.
- Provide plenty of time and encouragement.
- Expect to help out when children are feeling tired.

Moving out of nappies

There is no set time by which children will be ready to move out of nappies. In fact there is a huge range of normal development in this respect, with some children as young as twelve months being clean and dry while others may not be ready until closer to three years. (We will look at how best to support toilet training in Part 2, see page 118.)

Hand washing

Children will need to be helped to wash their hands for quite a while. It is not expected that children will be good at hand washing until they are three years. Even then, they will need adult help to dry their hands thoroughly. Expect to see children before this enjoying playing with water and soap rather than actually seeing hand washing as a process. In my experience, the soap dispenser is of particular interest to children and so its use may be a great motivator!

Getting it right

- Check that the water is not too hot.
- Talk to parents about whether their child has skin care needs, e.g. ordinary soap may be unsuitable for children who have eczema.
- Expect that two year olds will play as well as wash their hands.
- Model how to wash hands – especially how to interlock the fingers and make rotating movements.
- Check that children's hands are dry.
- Consider developing a song as part of the routine to make it more pleasurable.

Teeth cleaning

Children should have their teeth cleaned twice a day. It is not expected that children will be ready to clean their own teeth competently until they are seven years or so. Many young children want to clean their own teeth, but watch out for them just sucking the toothpaste and the brush! The compromise is to let them 'clean' their teeth first and then do the rest for them.

Mouthing

Mouthing is the need for babies and toddlers to explore objects using their mouths. Over time, mouthing decreases as children come to use their hands and eyes instead to explore items. Knowing whether or not children are still mouthing is important to prevent incidents of choking or swallowing items. It is also worth carrying out observation of new children carefully and asking their parents to see if they are mouthing. If a child is mouthing, consider buying a choke tube, which is a piece of plastic tubing that will allow you to judge whether an item is a potential choking hazard. Once children are no longer automatically mouthing, it means that smaller and potentially more challenging objects can be presented to them.

At what point should I refer a child who is still mouthing?

Consider referring a child who is still mouthing at two and a half years.

E. The two year old progress check

If you are working in England, there is currently a statutory requirement to carry out a progress check for two year olds. This check does not replace the assessments that you ordinarily carry out. It is expected that the requirements for this check may change, so do check the latest EYFS guidelines. In this section, we look at the purpose of the check and the practicalities of carrying it out.

Background to the progress check

It is worth understanding the background to the two year old progress check as it offers clues as to what exactly is required. In 2010 a report was commissioned that looked at children's life chances if they were born into economically poor families. The report, entitled *The foundation years: preventing poor children becoming poor adults* (Field, 2010), noted that even by 22 months, there were significant developmental gaps between children from poorer families and those from more affluent families. One of the conclusions drawn by the report was that there should be more funded places offered to children from disadvantaged families in quality early years settings – hence the two year old funded programme. In addition, it was decided that there should be a check on development when all children were two in order that any developmental delay could be picked up. The later Tickell review, which considered the EYFS, then focused on the importance of three prime areas to children's later school success: communication and language; personal, social and emotional development (PSED); and physical development (Tickell, 2010).

The future of the progress check

No one can gaze into the future and be sure of what is going to happen. The original idea of the two year old progress check was that it should be a combined health and education check. In some parts of the country, they have already piloted this. At the time of writing, parents are already invited to take their child for a two year old developmental check, so it does make sense to make these a combined check.

When to carry out the progress check

You are required to carry out a progress check on children in your setting between the ages of two and three years. The hope is that you will do the check close to the child's second birthday, but there is a legal requirement for you to agree the timing with the parent.

If children have already had their two year old progress check at another early years setting, you do not need to carry out another one. If a child attends two early years settings, you would need to agree with the parents which setting should complete it. Common sense would suggest that it would be the setting where the child spends the most amount of time, as they should be the best-placed to assess the child. (If you take children in at two or two and a half years, you may find that some parents think that the check has already been done. Some do not know that there is a difference between the health visitor-led check and this one!)

The two year old progress check should pick up children who may need additional support before they start school

What happens if a parent refuses to allow the two year old check?

This is mostly likely to occur when parents do not understand the purpose of the check. Do let parents know that this is not an 'exam' but more like a checklist. If parents are insistent that they will not allow the check to take place, ask them to put this in writing.

Getting it right

- Check that a two year old check has not been completed in another setting.
- Always agree the timing with parents.

Content

The legal requirement is to create a short written summary of the child's progress in three prime areas: personal, social and emotional development (PSED); communication and language; and physical development. You can choose to write about other aspects of the child's development including other areas of the EYFS or their interests, but only if you wish. You can also include photographs if you wish.

Personally, I would keep to what is required and make sure that the information is sufficiently in-depth. I would definitely advise this approach for anyone who already feels that they are burdened by paperwork. The statutory requirement clearly states it is a 'short written summary' so there is no need to write several pages.

The format

At the present time, no particular format is required and so you can draw up your own forms or download ones that are available online. The trick is to look at all the different ones available and make sure that you choose something that works for you. Never be afraid to adapt someone else's paperwork. You might like to look at A know how guide: the EYFS progress check at age two that can be found at www.gov.uk. It has several examples of paperwork that you can use as a starting point. It also makes some useful suggestions as to how to work with parents as part of this!

Information

You are required to write about how well the child is doing in each of the areas and you must write about strengths and clearly identify any areas where the child's progress is not typical for their age group. You could use the information in this book as well as from other sources, such as traditional milestones given in publications as well as from organisations such as I CAN. As the aim of the progress check is to identify delay and support that is then needed, it is important to use good sources of information. This way you can be confident of being accurate and able to justify your comments. I would also add that there is little point in making statements such as 'Is not yet sharing', as this is not age-related behaviour for two year olds. This type of statement can make parents feel that their child is not doing well. On the other hand, you must tell the truth about a child's development if they are behind the age-related stage (see Steps to take where a child is showing a delay, page 63).

After writing the summary

There is a legal requirement to *discuss* (not just write a letter) with parents how the summary of development can be used to support learning at home. As you are legally required to agree the timing with parents, it makes sense to arrange a time afterwards when you can discuss the summary.

Sharing the summary

You are supposed to encourage parents to share the summary with their health visitor or, where concerns have been raised about a child's development, to use it to gain a referral. When it is explained that the progress check will help others to work more effectively, most parents are happy to give their go ahead. They may also be happy for you to share it on their behalf.

What happend if a parent won't share information with other professionals?

Parents have the right not to pass on information to other professionals. The only time you can overrule this is where you feel that the child is in danger of abuse or being abused. If this were the case, you should follow the safeguarding procedures for your setting.

Steps to take where a child is showing a delay

Where a child is not showing expected development, not only do you have to write this down, but you are also required to create a targeted plan of action. The aim of the plan is to support children's future learning, which will show that you aim to involve other professionals where necessary. It is best practice to draw up the plan with parents and with a SENCO in group settings.

Requirements of the targeted plan

The EYFS states very clearly what should be included in the targeted plan. You have to show what activities and strategies will be put in place to support children's learning. If you already use individual education plans (IEP), you might like to use this format, but remember to attach it to the progress check summary.

How do I tell a parent that their child has a delay?

You should have already picked up that the child has a delay and have talked to parents about it. It is not good practice to wait for the two year old progress check to address your concerns with parents, as they may resent the fact that you have not brought it up before.

Can I refer a child without parents' consent?

No! While I recognise that this can be frustrating, some parents may not be ready to acknowledge that their child needs additional support. Respect that this might be the case, but let the parent know that they can revisit this decision at any time.

Supporting home learning

It is best practice to complete the progress check using information gained from observations in the setting, but also using information gained from parents. This is important because there is also a statutory requirement to give suggestions to parents as to how they might support their child's development at home.

The practicalities

For some settings that traditionally admit children just before their third birthday, taking in children who are barely two can come as a bit of a shock. If this is the case for your setting, you will need to adapt your provision and potentially your routines. On the other hand, if you have always had two year olds, it can be worth revisiting and evaluating your provision. This is particularly important if you work in England, where there are now more rigorous expectations in place. In Part 2, we focus on the practicalities of working with two year olds.

A. **Starting points**

B. **Creating an environment for personal, social and emotional development**

C. **Creating an environment for communication and language**

D. **Creating an environment for physical development**

E. **Creating an environment for two year olds' play**

A. Starting points

The funded two year old programme in England has meant that more two year olds are coming in to settings than ever before. Some of these two year olds may have developmental needs above and beyond those that are age-related. There are many things that are important to consider if you decide to increase the number of two year olds in your setting, especially those who have just turned two.

Considerations when taking on two year olds

If you are new to taking on very young two year olds, there are some things that are worth considering so that you are prepared.

- Do you have sufficient knowledge of the development of this age range?
- Have you risk assessed your setting with the younger age in mind?
- Are you equipped for this age's care needs, e.g. providing a place to sleep, potties?
- Do you have resources and equipment that will support two year olds' development?
- Are you familiar with the different ways that most two year olds play?
- Do you understand what is typical in terms of age-related behaviours, e.g. tantrums, sharing?
- Do you have good key person systems in place to prevent separation anxiety?
- If you work in home-based care, how might taking on additional two year olds affect your other children?

In addition, it is important to consider that some two year olds who come into the setting will not be showing age-related behaviours. This may be the case for some two year olds who have been referred by health visitors or social services, as these children may be assessed as being in need. For these children, you will need to identify their stage of development, which may of course be an earlier one to their actual age. Based on this, you will then need to ensure that your routines and practice meet their needs. Many children will need additional adult attention in order to thrive and make progress.

Are you ready for the new arrivals?

Two year olds alongside older children

For those of you working in group care settings, it is worth looking at how to manage mixed-age care. If currently you separate the two year olds from the older children, do look at the advantages of mixed-age care on the next page. On the other hand, if you work in home-based care, where this is less of an issue, feel free to skip to Working with parents (page 72).

One of the big dilemmas if you work in group care is whether or not you should have separate provision for two year olds, particularly those who have just turned two and/or are not showing expected development. Separate provision in group care can mean having separate rooms or, in large spaces, zoning off areas that are dedicated and staffed just for the two year olds.

In order to create an environment that meets all children's needs, it is worth exploring the advantages and the disadvantages of mixed-age groups. By understanding the advantages and particularly the potential disadvantages, it is possible to think about how to address them.

Advantages

- **Opportunities for older children to take on a nurturing role**
  Older children can develop a sense of responsibility and also gain in confidence from being with younger children. They gain the latter by seeing the difference between the younger children's skills and their own. They often adapt their play to incorporate younger children and are able to develop skills of empathy.

- **Wider opportunities and resources available for all children**
  Some settings find that by combining age groups, there is more space and resources available for all children. This may include the number of adults in the room. Two year olds in particular probably benefit the most from being able to access activities and resources that otherwise may not be thought of as being for their age group.

- **Opportunities for younger children to learn routines and skills from older ones**
  Two year olds often enjoy being with older children as they use them as role models. Many settings find that younger children soon learn about getting an apron for messy activities or washing their hands as they simply copy the older children.

These children are siblings and enjoy being together

- **The chance for siblings to be beside each other**
  Where children have siblings in the setting, especially if they spend
  a significant amount of time each week away from their homes,
  it makes sense that they should have opportunities to play and
  generally be together. Bonds made in childhood are important for
  later life and thought should be given to this. While some siblings may
  not play together, just knowing they are nearby can be comforting.

Disadvantages

There are, however, disadvantages to mixed-age groups worth noting:

- **Two year olds' play needs are different to older children's**
  This has to be recognised and we explore how their play is different
  in Factors to consider when planning a play environment (page 135).
  Sometimes older children can become frustrated because the younger
  ones are 'sabotaging' their play.

Most two year olds do not use role-play areas in the same way as older children

- **Routine group times may not work**
  Many group care settings have some organised group times such as
  circle time or story time. These are not likely to work for many two year
  olds because their language and attention skills are not likely to be
  sufficiently developed. This can mean that two year olds wander off or
  distract the other children.

- **Toys and equipment may not be suitable**
  Some toys and resources may not be safe for two year olds to play with as they may pose a choking hazard. Some toys are labelled as not suitable for the under-threes.

- **Behaviours**
  Behaviours that would be considered unwanted in older children are likely to be age-related and may be common in younger children. Staff may not always remember to adjust their expectations, and older children may feel that there is favouritism.

Risk assess toys that have this manufacturer's warning

- **Children may be overwhelmed by being in a large group**
  We saw in Part 1 that two year olds are likely to need to be close to an adult, preferably their key person. In large mixed groups, two year olds may not settle in if they are in a large space and not close to their key person.

- **Children may get fewer adult interactions as older children may 'jump in'**
  This last point is worth watching. We know that this is an important year in terms of two year olds' language development, as this is when most children move from two-word utterances to simple sentences. Where two year olds are in with older children, thought should be given as to how the adult–child ratio is used and whether it is the older children who actually benefit from the additional adults who are, in theory, there to support the younger ones.

Solutions

While there clearly are some disadvantages to mixed-age groups, there are some solutions that might be worth considering. Of course, a lot depends on the number of children that you are working with, the space that you have available and the layout. It is also important to take a flexible approach. Some two year olds will be close, either in age or developmentally, to being three years old and so separating them will not meet their needs.

- **Having some time for separate activities**
  This is a 'mix and match' approach whereby at some periods in the session older children engage in different activities or are in a different space to younger ones. This can work when there are group times or activities that are not safe or appropriate for the two year olds. Some settings retain a set time for stories or rhymes, but then split the children down into smaller age/stage groups so that the two year olds can have their needs met.

- **Creating separate areas for two year olds**
  Some settings create separate areas for younger children where they can retreat to if necessary and where specific activities and play opportunities might be set up. In some settings snack and meal times are taken in these areas so the key person can be sure to spend time with their key children.
- **Keeping the two year olds in small groups**
  Some settings organise part of their sessions so that the two year olds stay with or near their key person almost as if they were a little family. This can be quite nurturing for children who have just turned two or those who have just joined the setting.

Small groups can ensure that two year olds have sufficient adult attention

- **Monitoring systems**
  Some settings have monitoring systems during the session to ensure that the key person has spent time with their key children.

We were told that we have to use free flow in our setting. Is this true?

No, not in England. While the children must spend time outdoors, it is up to your professional judgement as to how best to organise your routines and setting.

Getting it right

- Develop monitoring systems to check how combining ages is working.
- Be aware that there may be some safety issues if children who are barely two also have developmental delay.
- Be flexible in your approach and ready to change groupings if necessary.
- Consider how siblings can spend time together.

Working with parents

Many parents of two year olds can find that this is a difficult period. As shown in Part 1, most two year olds are restless, active and likely to be clingy. In addition, parents can take the brunt of some of the age-related behaviours, such as temper tantrums. In England there is a new focus on helping parents to support their child's development at home. While it has always been good practice to work with parents to share ideas and thoughts about a child's care, learning and development, this is a further development.

How welcoming is your setting?

Getting off on the right foot

As we will see on page 82 about settling in, it is important that we get to know parents well and that a strong relationship is created from the start. First impressions definitely count, so do think about how welcoming your setting is and also how you intend to make parents feel that they can 'do business' with you. There may be some parents who have, for example, been 'told' that they must take the child to your provision in order to retain custody. These parents are not there voluntarily and so there are potential barriers to overcome. There will also be parents for whom you will be their child's first carers aside from family and friends. We therefore owe all parents our understanding and respect.

Open communication

One of the ways in which we can help develop a relationship with parents is to have very open communication. Saying something such as, 'I know from what you said that you were not looking forward to leaving Charlotte to go back to work, but we will do everything we can to make it work for you', tends to work better than not acknowledging a parent's feelings or body language.

Listening and learning

It is also important not to assume anything about what parents want, their lifestyles or their parenting beliefs. Early meetings with parents should bear this in mind and so 'listen and learn' is definitely a motto to be remembered.

Providing parents with information

While we need to learn from parents in order to work effectively, parents also need information. At first, this is likely to be information about what the setting does and how it works. While written policies should always be made available, many parents prefer to have verbal information as well. Asking parents what they would most like to know rather than bombarding them with information can work well right at the start, although you should always add in anything that is essential, such as that you have a no smoking policy or that children can only be collected by authorised adults.

Do we have to provide parents with a copy of every policy we have?

No, but they have to be available for parents. It would be sensible to give them a copy of any policy with information in it that would be useful on a day-to-day basis, e.g. about medicines or collection arrangements. Also, if you are a child minder in England, in theory you do not need written policies, although most child minders find having things written down avoids any misunderstandings.

Sharing information with parents about children's development

It has been best practice for a number of years to share information with parents about their child's development. There are of course a number of ways of doing this, but overall parents enjoy 'seeing' their child in action. Filming or taking photographs can work well, especially if we talk to parents about the significance of their child's behaviour. It is the understanding of what we have noticed that often helps parents to learn about their own child's development. Wherever possible, we should also be encouraging parents to feed back to us what they have seen their child do at home. Some settings set up secure links so that parents can send in photos of their child by email, while others routinely set aside time for updates (if you do decide to use technology, do make sure that you think about e-safety). Again, we have to be flexible in our approach.

Some parents may be in employment and so struggle to come in. Therefore, talking to parents about how best to communicate with them is essential. As well as talking to parents about their children's current development, it is also worth signposting what might be around the corner. This is a useful approach because it can help parents to have realistic expectations of their child's next steps. Where, for whatever reason, the child does not show the expected next step in development, it also means that it does not come as such a shock if we need to talk about this.

How honest should I be about a child's development?

Very! If you work with the EYFS, you have a duty to keep parents informed of their child's progress and also to flag up any concerns. Some practitioners, I suspect, are scared in case the reaction of parents is hostile, but any hostility is usually linked to parental feelings of protectiveness. It is important therefore that your communication style in such situations is friendly and demonstrates that you are clearly on the side of the child and the family.

Involving parents in supporting their child's development

This is the new focus for those settings following the EYFS. There are many ways of doing this and the best way is to get to know individual parents well. There is little point in telling parents that they should read a story at bedtime if you know that they work nightshifts or that they struggle with literacy. Settings that involve parents well are very sensitive to the parents that they work with and tailor suggestions accordingly. With some parents they may even provide the materials and resources so that a family who does not have any children's books can choose to take a couple. They also think about ensuring that any activity or developmental suggestion is likely to be successful. This is important when parents are doing things with their children for the first time. They may, for example, send a sound clip of a nursery rhyme that their child likes so parents can play it at home rather than just giving the parents the words. Settings that work well also talk to parents afterwards about how it went; it is important, however, to get the tone right so that parents do not feel judged.

It is important that ideas and resources for home learning are appealing

Getting it right

- Make sure parents understand the impact they can have on their child's development.
- Provide resources wherever possible as well as ideas.
- Provide an ideas board where parents can share ideas with each other as well as see those ideas put up by the setting.
- Gain feedback from parents on how the ideas and the support that you provide go.
- Recognise that parents have busy lives and sometimes other issues that mean that suggestions from us may not be given priority.

B. Creating an environment for personal, social and emotional development

The key person is the starting point for personal, social and emotional development, especially using the key person to settle the child in to the setting. In this section, we will look at these two elements in depth and discuss some tips for creating an environment that will support children's self-confidence and self-awareness. We will additionally discuss ways in which we might help children to manage their feelings and behaviour.

The role of the key person

To all intents and purposes, the relationship with the key person from the child's perspective should be akin to that of a favourite aunt or uncle.

A strong key person relationship is essential for children's well-being

As we saw in Part 1, two year olds show proximal attachment, meaning that the quality of children's key person relationship is essential for them to be settled and happy in a setting. They need their key person to be warm and fun, but also sensitive to their mood and needs. Two year olds are likely to want to stay close to their key person and if this relationship is not working well children are likely to become distressed, but also to miss out on opportunities for talk and learning. On the other hand, where the relationship is strong, children are keen to come into the setting and find 'their person'. They readily talk to their key person, want to show them things and involve them in their play.

The link between the key person and children's language development

Where children have a strong bond with their key person, they are more likely to do well with their language development. We saw in Part 1 that language develops rapidly between the ages of two and three, but also that it does need adult input. Where children are comfortable with their key person, they are more likely to seek to spend time with them and so gain more interaction. We also know that two year olds' early speech is not likely to be clear. This means that it becomes more important for children to be with adults who know them well, as they are much more likely to understand what the child is trying to say.

Checking the bond

It is important to check the strength of the key person bond, particularly in the weeks following the child's arrival. A strong key person relationship is active, not passive, in its nature. It is also not one-sided, where the adult is always the one to initiate communication. There should be some seeking behaviours, such as the child walking past another adult, determined that only their key person should help them, or the child noticing when the key person has moved position and duly seeking them out. Physical contact is also important.

We know that physical contact reassures children and reduces their anxiety. Children who have strong bonds will often seek out physical contact. They may unconsciously stroke the clothes or shoes of their key person or want to sit on their lap. It is also interesting to see that children may be cheeky when they have a strong bond with their key person. This is a good sign because it means that children are feeling relaxed.

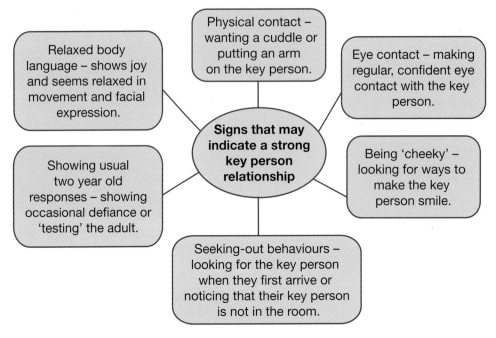

Relaxed body language – shows joy and seems relaxed in movement and facial expression.

Physical contact – wanting a cuddle or putting an arm on the key person.

Eye contact – making regular, confident eye contact with the key person.

Signs that may indicate a strong key person relationship

Showing usual two year old responses – showing occasional defiance or 'testing' the adult.

Being 'cheeky' – looking for ways to make the key person smile.

Seeking-out behaviours – looking for the key person when they first arrive or noticing that their key person is not in the room.

Signs that may indicate a strong key person relationship

Signs that the key person relationship is not strong

There are signs that a child might not be settled or that they do not have a sufficiently strong relationship with their key person. The obvious ones are that the child cries when they arrive, or parents report that they had difficulty in getting them to come in. You should also keep an eye out for children who after even a short break from the setting become very unsettled and need to be settled in again.

As well as obvious signs, you should also watch out for contrasts between how children behave when they are with their parents and how they behave in the setting. This could include a child who eats well at home but refuses anything in the setting, or who at home is toilet trained but has frequent accidents in the setting.

You should particularly look out for children who are scarily quiet and unusually obedient but who burst into emotion and life when their parents pick them up. This is worrying because it means that the child has been repressing all emotion in the interim. These children are often seen as being 'shy', when in reality they are actually in 'despair'.

What should you do if the child has not made a relationship with their key person?

The first step is to increase the amount of time that the key person and child are together. Create some simple routines so that the child knows what to expect, e.g. feeding the fish every day. Do not ask questions of the child, but simply 'be' with them and respond to what they are interested in. If after several sessions, the child still seems to be very unsure about being with the key person, it is worth changing key person and re-settling the child in using the 'Settling in without tears' approach outlined later in this section (see page 82).

What happens if a child develops a stronger relationship with another member of staff?

This can happen and it is important to be flexible. Provided that the member of staff does not have too many key children already, it would be simply a question of talking to the parents before moving the child across. If the member of staff already has their 'quota' of key children, then strategies should be put in place to build up the relationship between the child and their existing key person.

We normally wait and see who the child chooses?

If you work within the EYFS, there are legal requirements with which you must comply. The child's key person has to be allocated at the start and their role explained to parents. This prevents children from feeling 'lost', as there is an adult in place with responsibility for their emotional well-being. Common sense would dictate that if the child did not build a relationship, that a swap later on could take place.

Time matters

For the key person role to work well, children do need to spend sufficient time with their key person. For child minders this is usually not a problem, but in group care settings it is something that needs careful thought. Some settings build key person time into their daily routines, including:

- informal greetings/farewells
- key children sitting with their key person at snack and lunch time
- sharing a one-to-one or small group story with their key person
- personal care and nappy changing.

This is usually done in addition to children being able to access their key person at other times.

Other settings take a more flexible approach and have no set routine as such. If this approach is taken in large group settings, it is worth having a monitoring system to check that all children are accessing their key person regularly, as it is easy for some children to slip under the radar.

In terms of personal care, it is best practice for the key person or their 'back up' to be responsible. This is partly about children's dignity, as care such as nappy changing should never feel impersonal.

Getting it right

- Make sure that you have a strong key person system in place.
- Check that children have a strong bond with their key person.
- Think about how much time a child spends with their key person.

We operate a shift system and so there are times when a child's key person is not there.

Shift systems and part-time staff require a lot of organisational juggling. As children should never be without a key person, the secret is to have two adults acting as 'co-key persons', or 'buddying', as consistency is absolutely essential. Ideally, all children should have a second key person as a back-up, in case of the regular key person becoming ill or taking a holiday.

We are a mixed-age setting so in some sessions I have up to ten key children.

This is always difficult. I would begin by looking at which of the other adults do not have so many key children in those sessions. Then work out which of your key children (probably the older ones) do not need such intense support. Other adults could then focus on these children and thus become their co-key workers during your 'busy' sessions.

I am a child minder and need to take a week off work.

Many child minders have informal arrangements with other child minders to provide some continuity of care if they are ill or need to take some time off work. This can work well provided that the children have been introduced to the other child minder and have spent some time in their company. Drop in sessions or meeting at a play area are easy ways to help children become familiar with the back-up child minder. Parents will also need to know the back-up.

The key person role from the parents' perspective

The key person role is not just about caring for children; it is also about building a relationship with parents. This is particularly important in the EYFS, as key persons are expected to talk to parents about how they might support their child's learning at home. There is also a requirement in the EYFS for parents to be told about the role of the key person when their child starts in the setting.

To be an effective key person, it is worth understanding what parents are usually looking for. A search on the Mumsnet website is quite revealing. Most parents report that they want the child's key person to be someone that they can have confidence in and that they can trust to keep their child safe and happy. In group settings, parents tend to be concerned about whether anyone really 'knows' their child and is looking out for them. Parents also like to have feedback about what their child has done and for this to be sufficiently detailed so as to reassure them that the key person does have the measure of their child.

Getting it right

- Make sure that parents understand what a key person does.
- Show through your comments that you know their child well, and avoid vague comments such as 'He's had a good day.'
- Ask parents about their child at home and, if there are discrepancies, think about why this might be.
- Ask parents what information they would like to get about their child and how they would like to receive this, e.g. by email, daily slips, verbal exchanges.

Settling in

One of the most difficult aspects of working with two year olds is settling them in. In Part 1 we looked at attachment and the way that children are primed to stay close to their main care givers, usually their parents. We also saw that children are likely to become quickly distressed if they cannot see their parents. In this section, I want to give some suggestions for how to settle two year olds in and how, as part of this process, we might establish a strong rapport with parents.

Settling in without tears

For several years, I have been advocating a 'settling in without tears' approach to what is a huge transition for both children and parents. Settling in without tears works by ensuring that the child has had sufficient time to build a relationship with their key person before separation takes place. This might sound ambitious, but it is both efficient and effective.

There are five reasons why you should aim for this transition to be, literally, 'without tears'.

1 **Children's emotional well-being**
   When two year olds slip into separation anxiety and become distressed, their brains record this experience and an unconscious memory of it is stored. As a result, when the child experiences another transition, such as moving on to school or even having a change of key person, they will become very distressed. I would like to say that this is temporary, but the reality is that a two year old who has an 'unsuccessful' separation resulting in distress is very likely to struggle well into their teenage years. These are the children who dread changing class and whose parents report that they often have 'funny tummies' when they know that a supply teacher is coming in.

2 **Children's health**

Being away from home and their parents is stressful for children. This stress is reduced when children are with a key person. Without a strong bond, stress hormones in children's bodies are released in high quantities and these seem to suppress the body's immune system. This results in these children having a series of colds or other illnesses, while on the other hand children who have been settled in properly are more likely to be able to fight illness.

3 **Partnership with parents**

It is easy to forget, but separation affects parents, too. Settling in without tears as a way of working is a great way to build a relationship with parents and also to get to know each other. Parents who report leaving their children crying often comment that they found it hard to feel completely at ease with the staff who just told them to go!

4 **Effects on the setting**

Children who are distressed because they are not with their parents can affect the well-being of other children in the setting. It is deeply upsetting for children to hear others cry and this often leads to an otherwise settled child suddenly feeling anxious. It is also worth factoring in the amount of time 'lost' by staff who, rather than being able to interact positively and engage in play, are instead spending time making sure that the upset child is safe. This can disrupt the adult–child ratios and when settings add up how much time is spent trying to comfort an inconsolable child over what is likely to be a couple of weeks, they are often surprised that this can easily total twenty hours.

5 **Your setting's reputation**

Settling in without tears as an approach is great for your setting's reputation. We know that parents talk to each other and many places in settings are taken up by parents as a result of word-of-mouth recommendations. What can be more reassuring for a parent who is thinking about leaving their child with you than to know that this approach is being taken? Finally, you should also think about your inspection grade. All early years frameworks value quality relationships between children and adults. At the time of writing, it would be hard in England to gain an 'outstanding' grade if during an inspection there were children crying by the door, clearly upset. Indeed you might even find yourself in the land of gaining a 'notice to improve'.

Tricking nature

The starting point for settling in without tears is to understand that nature provided a very effective alarm system designed to keep children within sight or hearing of their parents or close family members. It is a great system. If, for one moment, a child cannot see their parent or family member, they start to cry loudly. This cry helps the parent to find them and so the child keeps crying until they are reunited with their parents. This is the 'protest' that I referred to in Effects of separation (page 12). The alarm system also affects parents, as firstly they are not meant to ever leave their child with a stranger or someone that they do not know well, and secondly they are of course meant to react to the child's cry. While this was a wonderful system when parents did not have jobs or require childcare, it has not been updated for modern-day living. Settling in without tears as an approach aims to trick nature into thinking that the key person is a member of the child's tribe, and so prevents nature's alarm system from ringing.

Before settling in takes place
Find out about the child's needs and experiences

The first step is to find out more about the child and his/her personality, and any previous experience of separation. This will give you an idea whether the child is likely to need longer to settle in or whether it is more likely to be straightforward. You can do this by having a structured form or you can simply ask a few questions. Do let parents know at the start that there are no right or wrong answers.

Familiarity with the setting can help younger siblings to settle

- How are parents feeling about leaving their child? You could ask them to rate this on a scale of 1 to 5, with 5 being very anxious.
- If there are older children in the family, how well did they settle into settings? (This question is useful because if parents have experienced difficulty with another child, they may be more concerned.)
- Has the child ever been left with a close family member or friend? If so, how did this go?
- Has the child ever been left at another setting, including a crèche? If so, when was this and how did the child react?
- How outgoing is the child? Does she tend to quickly get over any fear of strangers?
- How does the child show he is anxious, e.g. twiddling hair, thumb-sucking?
- Is the child out of nappies? If so, how established is this?

The information gained from parents should give you an idea whether a child is likely to need many settling-in visits before they are ready to be left or whether they can be 'fast tracked'. Children who can be 'fast tracked' are usually siblings of children already in the setting. These children are already familiar with you and once you are sure that they have a strong enough bond with you, they are unlikely to take long to settle.

Let parents know who you are

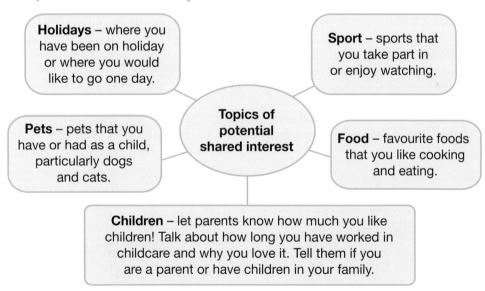

Holidays – where you have been on holiday or where you would like to go one day.

Sport – sports that you take part in or enjoy watching.

Pets – pets that you have or had as a child, particularly dogs and cats.

Topics of potential shared interest

Food – favourite foods that you like cooking and eating.

Children – let parents know how much you like children! Talk about how long you have worked in childcare and why you love it. Tell them if you are a parent or have children in your family.

Topics of potential shared interest

One of the most important things that can make a difference to settling in is whether or not parents feel that they like you and can trust you. Most parents are able to leave their children with family members, close friends and neighbours without worrying. While these people may not be qualified or even have had a background check, parents do this because they feel that they 'know' them. So first of all you need to help parents find out more about you as a person. There are many ways of doing this, including creating a personal profile or having a box of items that reflect your life. Communicating and sharing interests with parents, about pets for example, can make a huge difference, as if they too have a pet you are likely to exchange stories about them. In the same way, if you support a football team or enjoy a certain food, you are likely to be able to make a connection. The best way to approach this is to help parents feel that you are 'human' and 'approachable', while not giving away information that might be too personal or inappropriate.

Explain the settling-in process to parents

Using the information provided by the parents, the next step is to talk through the process of how the child is to be settled in. They need to know that you and they will be working together to settle the child in and that there are five steps to the process. Their role during the process is to gradually withdraw while your role is to build a relationship. It can be useful to write out the steps with an explanation of what parents need to do at each stage.

It is a good idea to let parents know that while it usually takes three visits to settle children in, the speed depends on how quickly the relationship with the child develops. Where a child has had an 'unsuccessful' separation, the pace might be much slower and indeed it might be worth also adding in a home visit. For parents who wish to return to work or have an urgent schedule, it is worth suggesting that additional 'incidental visits' are scheduled in alongside the settling-in visits.

What should we do if a parent refuses to do settling-in visits?

To avoid this type of situation, state in your admissions policy that settling-in visits are a requirement, and talk about the value and importance of settling in when parents first come to view your setting or enquire about a place.

If a parent is adamant that they will not stay, you could also explore why they feel this way. It may be that they do not realise the implications of their rushing off, or that they have previously had a bad separation experience and so prefer to 'cut and run'. For some working parents, it may be that the settling-in visits will mean taking time off work. In this case, you could explore whether another family member or close friend that the child knows well could take their place in the settling-in or look for more flexible times. You should also let working parents know that when children are settled and happy, they are less likely to be ill or have a 'funny tummy' as a result of childcare changes.

We normally tell parents to stay and play until the child is ready to let them leave.

This approach is fine as it is child-led, but it may not always be the most efficient. Some parents report that they find themselves staying for several weeks. Their children enjoy their parents' undivided attention so much that they are reluctant to let them go. If you use this approach, it is important that the child spends time playing with their key person too so that the relationship is built up, and also that the parent is encouraged to increasingly take a 'back seat'.

The five-step process

This five-step process works by allowing children to get to know us and helping them to see the key person as someone they can trust as their parent gradually withdraws. Each step is practised until it is fully mastered and only then is the next one tackled. If at any point children look unsure, return to the preceding step. As parents have an active role in this process, make sure that they know what they have to do for each step and agree a cue. The five steps are as follows:

1 **The child plays with the key person when the parent is available**
   This step begins by the parent, key person and child all engaging in a play activity. Using an agreed cue, the parent starts to withdraw eye contact and picks up a magazine. The step is repeated until the child can make eye contact with and continue to play happily with the key person.

2 **The child plays with the key person as the parent wanders across the room then returns immediately**
   This is an important step for children who have never been left before, as it helps them to see that parents may go but they always come back. Once the key person and the child are happily playing, on cue, the parent wanders a few feet away before immediately returning. It is worth putting out a few books or magazines so that there is a purpose to their wandering. Repeat until the child does not seem bothered.

3 **The child plays when the parent moves in and out of sight in the room**
   This is a development from the previous step. Once the child is settled and playing with the key person, on cue, the parent pops out of sight (but stays within the room). Cupboards come in handy for this. Again, repeat this step until the child does not break off their play.

4 **The child is happy to stay with the key person when the parent goes out of the room for one minute**
This step can take time for parents and children to master, but is important because it helps parents learn to say goodbye while teaching children that their parent always comes back. Once the child is settled and playing with the key person, the parent tells the child that they are popping out for some tea (or something else that is in the child's immediate interest). It is important parents know that they must sound confident and go immediately, showing no hesitation (some parents may need to practise a script). The parent then moves very purposefully towards the door, picks up the agreed object and then immediately returns. Expect that for the first few times, children will stop playing with the key person and start instead to follow the parent. Do not restrain children but accompany them, saying 'It's okay. Mummy/Daddy is just getting you something.' Repeat until the child is looking more confident.

5 **The child is happy to stay with the key person when the parent leaves for ten minutes. The child is comfortable with some physical contact, e.g. hand-holding**
The final step is a development on the previous step. The parent announces that they are 'popping out' but the amount of time spent out of the room increases.

Getting it right

- Agree beforehand a cue to indicate that parents need to take an action.
- Repeat each step until the child seems unfazed.
- Expect that some steps will require more practice.
- Recognise that some parents find it hard to 'step back' from their children.

Physical contact

During the settling-in process, the key person should also be building up opportunities to offer the child physical contact. This might start by offering a toy or something that a child takes from your hand. By step 5, you need to be sure that the child will hold your hand or allow you to give them a hug. This is important because if later on the parent leaves and the child becomes upset, we need to be able to offer them a cuddle. Cuddling is important because research indicates that it reduces the amount of stress hormone that the child produces when they are upset. Having said this, cuddling only works if the child is comfortable with the adult – otherwise, it can actually increase the child's stress.

In the comforting presence of his mother, this child is getting to know his key person

Toileting

Some children quickly settle in, but become concerned about having their nappy changed or, if they are toilet trained, about going to the toilet. As part of the settling-in visits, make sure that they have experienced this. You can, for example, agree with parents that you will both accompany the child to the toilet, or they will start off a nappy change but you will finish it off. Toilet training is discussed in greater detail later in Part 2.

What type of activities should we use for these settling-in visits?

Look out for activities that allow the child to participate and will allow you to play together. You can ask parents for their ideas. Bubbles, for example, are useful because children enjoy catching them and this is something that you can do together. Simple ball games can also work well, as can bringing out a puppet. Avoid anything that is so intriguing for children that they totally ignore you to concentrate on it.

I am worried as we have a child coming soon who does not speak any English.

First, get organised. Take some photographs of key areas and people within your setting and laminate them on to some cards. This will mean that the child and their parent will be able to point to things. You can also buy resources that have talking pens. When pointed at a picture, these will say the word or sentence in the relevant language. In terms of settling in, allow much longer to settle the child in so that they really are confident with their key person before any separation takes place.

Home visits

Home visits can help children and their parents to get to know their key person

Home visits are a great way to get to know children and their parents and can be a good way to fast track the settling-in process. They are especially useful if parents and children have previously had a bad experience or if parents are very nervous. It can be helpful to ask the parent to take a photograph of you and the child together so that when you meet the child again, you or the parent can remind the child that you have already met.

Incidental visits

Some children who have had a bad experience or who parents tell us are very shy may need to meet us several times before actually starting the settling-in process. It can be a good idea to ask parents to 'drop by', or if you are a child minder to let parents know where you are likely to be on any given day, e.g. at a drop-in session or a school pick-up, so they can arrange a brief meet. These brief incidental visits can help children to become familiar with their key person before settling in begins.

> **A child is coming to us who did not settle at their previous nursery.**

> When you know that a child, and most likely a parent, has had a bad experience, it is important to take the settling-in process gently. You might also like to add in a home visit and also a few incidental meetings for good measure.

> **Is there a best place for settling in?**

> Two year olds who are unsure often feel more relaxed in larger spaces, especially outdoors where they feel less trapped. If the weather is good, consider following the steps outdoors.

> **We operate termly and normally do the settling-in in the last week of the term, then the children come in when we start the new term in the autumn. Some of the children seem to 'forget' over the summer.**

> This is not ideal, and while you could start the settling-in during the last week of term, consider resuming settling in for the first week. You might also like to think of strategies to keep the memory of being in the setting alive for the child. This could include sending home a photograph of the child and their key person for the parents to show to the child from time to time, as well as sending a couple of postcards to the child during the summer.

Is it possible to settle more than one child in at a time?

Yes and it can work well, provided that the parents feel comfortable together. You will need to make sure that you spend time focusing on each child separately, though, and you may need to think about activities that you can set up where children can easily play in parallel.

Self-confidence and self-awareness

In Part 1, we saw that children's self-confidence and self-awareness is very much in development. The role of the key person and how well children are settled in is critical to this aspect of development. Children who are relaxed and settled in the absence of their parents are likely to enjoy exploring and

Through her body language, this key person is showing that she values this child

accessing resources, play opportunities and activities. Unsettled children, on the other hand, are likely to be preoccupied by the absence of their parents. They may not therefore try anything new or even engage in play opportunities and activities.

The key person role is also essential because children learn about themselves from others' body language, interest and words. Where there is a strong relationship, children will see that they are liked, respected and valued. This is sometimes referred to as the 'looking glass effect', whereby children learn about themselves from how they see others respond to them.

Comforters

Many two year olds will need a comforter, especially when they first start at a new setting. Comforters are items that children use to help them cope with stress. Typical comforters include a small cuddly toy, a blanket or even a strip of fabric. Dummies are also comforters (see page 100). It is a good idea to be flexible with the use of comforters until such time as children are settled in and can be properly comforted by their key person. Denying a comforter to an upset child is never good practice.

Routines for self-confidence and self-awareness

Children can gain in confidence when they are empowered to do things independently. It is important to look at the routines that we create for children so as to ensure that they are able to do things as independently as possible. This means looking for opportunities for children to choose play opportunities and to access resources, but also looking at how we help children to gain self-care skills. We look in depth at self-care on page 106, as self-care skills are so important.

Managing feelings and behaviour

Again, we have to consider the role of the key person as fundamental in supporting the management of feelings and behaviour. Children who have a strong relationship with their key person are more likely to be emotionally stable, although they will still show the usual age-related behaviours such as rapid changes of mood.

In Impulsivity in Part 1 (page 22), we looked at the way in which children's emotional regulation and impulsiveness is likely to affect how well they can cope with feelings and behaviour. We also looked at how best to manage typical age-related behaviours including biting and tantrums. In terms of creating an environment that will help children, it is important to think firstly about routines. We know that hunger and tiredness are very problematic and will affect children's potential for managing their feelings and behaviour. Routines have to be developed with this in mind and flexibility must also be built in, as children may become hungry at different times, depending on when they were last fed, and equally will become tired at other times, too. As tiredness has such an impact on children's ability to manage their feelings, we look in depth at sleep and napping on in Sleep (page 124).

As well as considering tiredness and hunger, we also need to think about creating an environment that whenever possible removes potential sources of frustration. We know, for example, that children who are just two find it hard to wait, and so making sure that things are ready for them can reduce potential frustration. We also know that children find it hard to understand why they cannot have something that they can see. It makes sense therefore to remove things from children's sight line that they cannot have, including, for example, dummies if these are only to be used at nap time (see the Questions and concerns speech bubble on page 100).

Avoiding conflict

Most settings that have few conflicts or issues with behaviour with their two year olds do so because they are good at creating environments that remain stimulating and reflect the way that this age group plays. We look at how to do this in Factors to consider when planning a play environment (page 127). A final, but important, tip in helping children to manage their feelings and behaviour is to make sure that they have plenty of time outdoors. Being outdoors is very empowering for children. It is also stimulating, as there is plenty to see and discover even on a walk around the neighbourhood. We know that physical activity stimulates chemicals in the brain that enhance positive emotions. This is why, if you audit the situations in which your two year olds are the happiest and where there are fewest incidences of frustration, you may find that these correspond with children being outdoors.

Getting it right

- Check that the key person relationship is strong.
- Talk to parents about when their child usually sleeps.
- Keep an eye out for signs of tiredness or hunger.
- Build into your routine plenty of outdoor activity.
- Look for opportunities to empower children through play and self-care.
- Avoid over-reacting to age-related behaviours.

C. Creating an environment for communication and language

We saw in Part 1 that children's communication and language skills will develop rapidly during this year. It is therefore important that environments are created to support this area of development.

Key person role

It is essential that every two year old has a strong relationship with their key person. Not only is this important for the emotional well-being and confidence of the child, but it is essential for their communication. Two year olds' communication and language is closely linked to the amount of quality adult interactions they receive and how motivated they are to communicate. Children who are comfortable and enjoy being in the company of their key person are likely to spend longer talking and communicating, and so their language development is likely to progress well. It is therefore worth thinking about how much key-person time is available for Communication and Language. This might be simply playing alongside a child or sharing a story with them.

Background noise

Background noise is likely to make it harder for children to listen easily. Interestingly, it also seems to affect children's motivation to speak. The best setting layouts are therefore ones that provide some small cosy spaces. In home-based care, background noise tends not to be an issue as there are often fewer children and the physical space tends to be smaller. Having said that, having a radio or a television on, even in the background, or there being another source of background noise, can reduce communications. If you work in group care, you might like to look at your layout carefully. Large rooms, especially with high ceilings, can be problematic. Think about moving furniture out so that it is adjacent to the wall. You might consider looking for rugs to absorb sound. There is also the option of looking at soundproofing materials that can be stapled on to the walls. Finally, remember not to have the radio turned on.

Small spaces seem to cut down background noise

Time for quality interactions

In terms of creating an environment that supports communication and language, the focus has to be on building a routine that allows for quality interactions. Two year olds primarily need to be given undivided adult attention. Ideally, this should be one-on-one interaction, but this will not of course be possible all of the time. There are some features of quality interaction that seem to be significant. These should be the focus of any self-evaluation. Interestingly, the level of interaction and its quality is something Ofsted and the other inspectorates evaluate carefully.

Time

Two year olds need sufficient time to process what they want to say and also to respond to our comments or questions. They are also likely to talk more when they sense that adults are not in a hurry to move on, and so sitting down or getting to their level is important.

Style

The style of our interactions is important. Avoid speaking loudly or sharply, as two year olds respond to warm sing-song tones. It is also important to be sensitive and to avoid drowning children in a sea of continual comments and questions as children need time to process what is being said. Too much talk by adults often results in children not saying very much. This is particularly worth remembering when a child is engrossed in play or is finding something fascinating. It is also thought that overcorrecting children can hinder their development. It is therefore better to model correct grammatical language and use a technique known as 're-casting'. This technique involves acknowledging what a child has said and repeating back as part of conversation what the child said, but in correctly formulated grammar or pronunciation.

Getting it right

Consider recording yourself as you interact with children. Look at whether you:

- listen to and acknowledge children's speech
- give children sufficient time to respond and process
- expand on what children are trying to say
- indirectly model correct grammar or pronunciation by repeating back what children say.

Using the outdoor area

It is important to build plenty of outdoor time into your routine. Not only does this seem to help children to manage their feelings and behaviour, but children are often more comfortable talking when they are outdoors. Walks, for example, can encourage children to chat about what they are seeing as children often sense that they have the undivided attention of 'their adults'. Interestingly, many adults working in home-based care report that walking to and from school to collect older charges is often a language-rich moment with their two year olds – even though the pace of the walk is slow!

In group care settings, using outdoor areas fairly continuously makes good sense as it is a way to avoid noisy indoor environments while also again providing a rich environment for talk. Do think, though, about providing for cosy environments outdoors. Willow frames, tents or even playhouses seem to encourage communication.

Providing sufficient interaction

With the exception of home-based care, two year olds in England are likely to be on a 1:4 ratio, although slightly higher ratios exist in some other home nations such as Scotland. These ratios should allow for plenty of individual attention, which is exactly what two year olds need in order to progress their communication and language. If you have your two year olds in with older children, think about whether it is the older children who are benefitting from the additional adults in the room. Some two year olds are much quieter when there are older children around, partly because the older children interrupt often or are more adept at getting attention. It is therefore worth thinking about how you might organise the routine to ensure that there are times when younger children can 'get their say'. This might be through the use of key person time or in the case of home-based care through maximising language opportunities when the older children are absent or engaged in their own activity.

We have some older children who tend to take over. It seems unfair to tell them to go away.

All children need quality attention so this has to be the starting point. Think firstly about whether the older children are getting sufficient time. Then in those periods when you wish to focus on the two year olds, think about what there is available for the older children to do. Sometimes older children want to become involved because what we are doing with younger children is more interesting than what is available to them. If an older child's speech is good, there is no harm in gently telling them that they may have to wait but you will have some time for them later, and directing them to a play opportunity.

Stories

It is important also to build stories into the daily routine. Stories are important in developing children's communication and language. They provide opportunities to learn new vocabulary and sentence structure, and also to improve listening skills. Most two year olds enjoy looking at books, although they will struggle in a large group story. This is because they need the close proximity of an adult in order to maintain attention as well as needing to examine the pictures. This means that the most effective way of sharing stories with this age group is ideally to do so individually or in pairs. This allows children to snuggle in, follow the story and talk about it. Adults working with children also find it easier to share books this way because children's attention does not stray and it doesn't matter if children want to go back and look at a preceding page. This means that sharing books should be a priority in terms of the routine of the setting.

Choosing books

There are no 'wrong' or 'right' books, but the secret to choosing a book is firstly to make sure that you like it! When adults read a book that they love to children, they tend to use richer voice tones, they also spend longer looking at the pictures with children and their enthusiasm conveys itself to the child. On the other hand, where adults read a book that they don't like, they tend to skip pages, read with a flatter voice and hurry to get to the end! This means that it is worth looking at the books that you have available in your setting and considering whether they are sufficiently enjoyable.

As well as ensuring that you like the book, you should also make sure that the book links closely to the child's language level. Think about the level of book that you need – for example, will you need the type of book characterised by the 'Spot the Dog' series with single repetitive sentences on each page, or a book with an involved story line? Books that contain repetition are particularly useful as they allow children to anticipate the sentences and eventually join in.

This child is gaining more from this activity because the adult loves this book

Rhymes and songs

These also need to be built into the routine of the setting. They are considered important in building children's phonemic awareness, which is needed for later reading and writing. The great thing about rhymes and songs is that children find them enjoyable and that older and younger children can do them together. In terms of best practice, you should consider planning rhymes and songs to make sure that children have the opportunity to develop a wide knowledge of them. Look out for:

- action songs, e.g. 'Head, Shoulders, Knees and Toes'
- action rhymes, e.g. 'Pat-a-cake'
- finger rhymes, e.g. 'Two Little Dickie Birds'
- traditional nursery rhymes, e.g. 'Tom Thumb'
- counting rhymes, e.g. '1, 2, 3, 4, 5, Once I Caught a Fish Alive'.

Getting it right

- Aim that each day a child has a shared story with their key person.
- Observe which books individual children seem to enjoy and repeat.
- Look carefully at the quality of the books in your setting.
- Plan rhymes and songs so that children can keep learning them.
- Observe which rhymes and songs particularly appeal to individual children.
- Listen out for children repeating rhymes and songs by themselves.

Many of our two year olds are reliant on dummies.

Dummies can affect children's communication. Firstly, in order to talk properly, children have to make the effort to remove the dummy from their mouth. This often reduces the amount of communication. In addition, children's ability to smile and show a range of facial expressions is limited if they have a dummy in their mouth. This can act as a barrier to the communication cycle. It is worth therefore having a policy whereby dummies are only used for comfort when a child is upset or to help them sleep. Once a child has settled in, gradually 'wean' the child off the dummy by, for example, having a 'five minute out, five minute in' policy. The amount of time the child spends without the dummy increases. This only works when the child is not tired and also when what they are doing is so fascinating so that they do not notice the absence of the dummy. It is also important to work with parents on this. It may be important to inform some parents that it will be harder for their child to make friends if they have a dummy (because of the reduced facial expression).

I have a child whose parents speak Japanese at home.

What a lucky child to have access to two languages! Children have the ability to learn more than one language provided they are sufficiently exposed to them and so there is no problem as such. The received wisdom is to encourage the child's parents to continue with Japanese at home and for you in the setting to use English. If the child is new to your setting, think about using plenty of visual cues and pictures to make communication easier. You will also need to make sure that there is a strong relationship between you and the child, and that you provide plenty of opportunities for enjoyable interaction.

D. Creating an environment for physical development

All areas of development are interlinked. Already we have seen that there are strong links between the role of the key person and the development of Communication and Language. We have also seen that being outdoors supports children's language and their ability to manage their feelings and behaviour. In this section we focus on the ways in which we can create an environment that will support children's movements, both large and small. This is the basis of moving and handling within the EYFS. We then go on to consider aspects of self-care in some depth, as this is the area where children will make significant progress over the year as they approach three.

Large motor movements and coordination

We saw in Part 1 that it is part of normal development for two year olds to be active and restless. It is important therefore to build movement into their daily routines. Ideally children need to be given a chance to play outdoors in addition to having opportunities to go for a walk. This is particularly important if your outdoor area is small in order to ensure that children are having enough vigorous physical activity. Being able to go for a walk is also, as we have seen, great in terms of stimulating children.

Resources and equipment

A lot of children's large motor activity comes from their play, which we will be looking at in Recognising play patterns (page 132). We know that children this age like to climb, kick and move things. It is therefore important to do an audit to check that you have sufficient resources to provide for a range of opportunities. Following is a checklist you might like to use to consider whether you have a wide enough range of opportunities available.

Activity	Resources	Available?
Balancing	Seesaws, swings, climbing frames, low walls, beams, scooters	Y/N
Climbing	Wooden logs, climbing frames, tyres	Y/N
Throwing and catching	Bean bags, soft balls, cuddly toys	Y/N
Kicking	Plastic footballs	Y/N
Walking and running	Reasons to do so, e.g. catching bubbles	Y/N
Pushing, pulling and steering	Wheelbarrows, pushchairs, sit-and-ride toys	Y/N
Pedalling	Tricycles	Y/N

Checklist of resources

Encouraging physical movement

It is important to recognise that physical activity must be enjoyable. Play is usually a great motivator and many children will happily want to move around. Some children, however, may need encouragement from adults. Look out for things to do with children, such as blowing bubbles for them to catch or encouraging them to sweep up some leaves in the autumn. Some children may also be wary of new experiences, especially if they have had a negative experience such as a fall. It is therefore important to stay close with them and if necessary lend a helping hand. It is important never to push children beyond their comfort zone. Being stressed is likely to hamper children's coordination.

A helping hand can support children's progress

103

Fine motor movements

There is a real link between children's fine motor movements, including their hand–eye coordination, and their confidence. These movements enable children to tackle tasks, including feeding and some level of dressing, that allow them to be independent of adults. To support fine motor movement, you need to look at everyday activities as well as play opportunities that will support a range of movements.

Tidying, cleaning and washing

Most two year olds enjoy helping adults. Tidying, cleaning and washing are great ways to help children to develop some fine motor movements. Tidying could include taking their plate or cup to a sink ready for washing up, as well as traditional tidying away of toys. Simple cleaning tasks, such as using a dustpan and brush or wiping a table, encourage children to make accurate movements. Giving children a toothbrush or some building blocks as a washing activity provides opportunities for two-handed movements of the kind that support development of hand preference (see Handedness, page 51).

Two year olds love helping adults

Planning play opportunities

While many play opportunities automatically prompt children to make a range of hand movements, it is worth auditing what is available to ensure that each day children have the opportunity to practise a range of hand movements. The table below gives examples of hand movements with suggestions of resources and play opportunities you could use to audit your provision.

Movement	Resource/opportunity	Available?
Pincer grasp	Threading Finding and picking out small objects Picking up small items with tweezers Peg boards	Y/N
Strengthening of hands	Sponges in water Playdough Gloop (mixture of cornflour and water) Rolling pins Twisting lids off bottles	Y/N
Finger isolation (using individual fingers)	Finger painting Finger rhymes Keypads and gadgets Making shapes in gloop	Y/N
Hand arches (helps the hand curl, freeing the thumb and index finger to be more precise)	Scooping movements, e.g. in sand, water Twisting caps on and off Tongs, tweezers and spinning tops	Y/N
Strengthening hand preference (each hand working but involved in different tasks)	Dustpan and brush Beating a drum with two sticks Using a spoon and fork Threading beads or pasta Tearing strips of paper Doing up buttons Pouring from one container into another	Y/N
Hand–eye coordination	Any movement requiring a level of precision Painting Small world play Jigsaw puzzles Building towers of bricks or using construction toys Threading Simple sewing cards for older two year olds	Y/N

Examples of hand movements

Getting it right

- Make sure that your daily routine encourages a range of large and small movements.
- Audit your resources and planning to ensure that play opportunities will develop a range of small movements.
- Think about how you might check that children are practising movements.

Self-care

Two year olds need a lot of support with their personal care, from dressing through to nose blowing and toilet training. They also need opportunities to master and practise the skills of personal care both at home and in the setting. It is always interesting to see the way that mastering some of the skills associated with self-care gives children confidence. This is because being able to do things without waiting for others is empowering and gives children a 'can do' attitude. Self-care is of course part of any routine involving this age group, but it is important that sufficient time is built into the routine to empower children.

Dressing

In Self-care skills at different ages in Part 1, page 55, we saw that two year olds' dressing skills are still very much in development. They will need opportunities to practise skills such as taking off jumpers and putting on shoes and coats. Between the ages of two and three, this will become increasingly easier as their hand–eye coordination develops. Ideally, this is an area where we should work with parents so that once a child gains or is developing a skill, they are given opportunities to master it at home or in the setting.

Undressing is often easier at first than dressing

Supporting children's dressing skills

When organising the environment and developing routines to help children develop their dressing skills, the main thing is to recognise that for many tasks, such as putting on shoes, trousers and even jumpers, they do better

Managing buttons	Practise threading activities. Look out for large buttons on stretchy fabric, e.g. dress teddy. Talk children through the process of using buttons, e.g. first find the button, now find the hole. Create some fabric bags for toys that have large buttons and buttonholes on them so children can practise every day.
Zips on garments, e.g. coats	With the agreement of parents, put some ribbon through the zipper and tie it so as to make a loop. This will make it easier for the child to hold and pull the zip up and down.
Socks	Start with children pulling off their socks. Get children to sit against the wall as this can help for stability. Pull the sock over their toe and heel and let them pull up the rest.
Coats	There are a couple of methods – agree with parents which one to use. Model it with children. 1 Put a child's coat on to the chair they are sitting on. See if they can find the arms of the coat and slip their arms into the coat before standing up. 2 Lay out the coat on the floor on its back, with the front facing up. Turn it away from the child so that the neck is nearest to them. Encourage the child to put their arms through the arms of the coat. Then tell the child to stand up and flip the coat over their head (see page 108).
Shoes	Begin by encouraging children to take off their shoes. To help children get the right shoe on the right foot: With the agreement of parents, you can add a sticker such as a star on to one shoe and have a laminated card that has the outline of two shoes – one of which has a star on it. Children then match the shoes on to the card.
Trousers	Trousers require a significant amount of balancing and so expect that children will need significant help. With children standing up, undo the zip and button of the trousers. Encourage them to push them down before sitting and removing them.

Supporting children's dressing skills

sitting or kneeling on the floor. This means that if you do not have sufficient space in the hallway or in a cloakroom, it is worth children collecting things and taking them to where there is some floor space. I have seen dressing baskets used for this purpose, which worked well and also helped in the battle to keep things tidy. Dressing takes time and this should also be factored into the routines of the day.

One of the methods for teaching a two year old to put on their coat

We encourage children to take off their own coat in the morning, but some parents insist on doing it for their children.

Caring and 'babying' children is an expression of love and many parents do this as part of their 'goodbye' routine, so I would personally not interfere. On the other hand, I would separately provide information to parents that shows the link between self-care skills and children's confidence levels. You might also link it to children's later handwriting skills.

Skincare

Unless you are working as a nanny or providing overnight care, the amount of skincare that you need to provide is probably limited to hand and face washing. As with other areas of children's care, it is important to work with parents to make sure that individual children's needs are met. This is particularly important in terms of children who may have skin conditions or where parents have particular preferences, which may in some cases be linked to their culture or religion.

Hand washing

Hand washing plays a major role in preventing illness and the spread of infection. In this year many children will move towards being able to independently wash their hands and it is vital that they develop this as a habit. Children are more likely to learn to enjoy washing their hands if the environment is attractive and properly equipped. Make sure that children can easily access a sink at their level as well as soap and towels. It is good practice in group settings to prevent the spread of infection to provide paper towels or small individual hand towels that can be laundered later. It is also important that a set routine is established for key hand washing moments such as before lunch and after visiting the toilet.

Using a step-by-step guide

It can be helpful to put a step-by-step pictorial guide to hand washing so children can see the sequence, from pushing back sleeves to turning off taps and drying hands. You can then point to each picture as you move through the stages with children. As you observe children developing some of the skills, you can then point to the stage and ask them to do it independently. A lovely touch is to create the step-by-step guide by photographing children in your setting showing each of the different steps.

Hand washing has to be enjoyable so that it becomes a habit

Avoid rushing

For two year olds, a thing such as a soap dispenser or even soap is something to be explored. Allowing time for children to enjoy the process is important, as children are more likely to develop positive attitudes towards it rather than seeing it as a chore.

Role modelling

One of the ways that two year olds can learn about hand washing is by watching adults. This means that you should take your time when washing your own hands, use soap and take time to dry them. It is often the drying stage that adults skip over by simply wiping their hands, and children are more likely to copy this.

Face washing

After meals, most two year olds, especially those who have just turned two, will need their faces cleaning. This should be something that they can do independently. A good tip is to have a portable mirror or to take children to a bathroom mirror. This way they can see why they need to wash their face and can also see where they need to wash their faces. Damp cloths, one per child, or face wipes are usually used. As children's faces can become chapped, you should also think about providing soft towels so that children can dry their face. As with hand washing, individual towels should be provided to minimise the spread of infection.

We have a child who has eczema and is not allowed to use soap.

Soap can dry out skin and so is often not recommended for children with eczema or other skin conditions. It is, however, worth talking to parents about alternatives and asking whether moisturising cream should be applied after washing hands.

Nose blowing

Children need to learn how to blow their nose effectively as a blocked nose can affect the clarity of children's speech. It is also unpleasant for the child and others around them to have a runny nose. To encourage children to blow their nose, it is important that tissues are easily available and ideally put in several different places in the setting. It is worth putting bins near the 'tissue' station so that children get into the habit of blowing their nose and then disposing of the tissue into the bin. It is also worth making sure that tissues are put in attractive boxes to help to motivate children. Some settings also help children get into the habit of blowing their nose promptly by having a sticker chart. This is worth trying if you have children who are reluctant.

Tips for teaching nose blowing

As with other skills, children need to be taught how to blow their nose. Interestingly, this skill is best taught when children do not have a cold. There are a few stages to teaching children about blowing their noses.

Step 1 Begin by playing games that involve blowing through the mouth
You can use bubbles or strips of tissue paper to see if they can make them move, or roll up tissue balls and see if they can send them across a table. Move on to step 2 when they seem to understand the word 'blowing'.

Step 2 Model blowing through the nose
Show children that with your mouth shut, you can blow through your nose. Put a strip of tissue paper or crêpe paper in front of your nose and, with your mouth shut, blow and make it move. Make sure that children see you have your mouth closed, and that you remind them of this.

Children need to learn what it feels like to blow through their nose

Step 3 Play games where children are blowing through their nose
See if children can gently blow through their nose and make a tissue paper strip move, as you did in step 2. Play other games, e.g. rolling a small bit of paper into a ball and seeing if children can make it move. Always remind children to close their mouth when blowing through their nose.

Step 4 Blowing through the nose with one nostril gently blocked
See if the child can repeat step 3, but with one nostril gently blocked. Children can either put a finger against the nostril or you can do this gently for them.

Step 5 Blowing through the nose without the need for a resource
See if children can repeat steps 3 and 4 without the need for a resource or game. Check that they can do this by putting your hand under their nostril.

If children are able to manage these steps, they will have developed the concept of blowing through their noses and so when they have a cold, it will be easier for them to gently remove the mucus. It is worth sharing these steps with parents so that they can practise them with the child too.

Getting it right

- Make sure there are plenty of places where children can independently access tissues.
- Role model blowing your own nose, putting the tissue in the bin and washing your hands afterwards.
- Remind children to place used tissues in the bin.
- Teach children about nose blowing when their nose is not blocked.

We have one child who seems to constantly have a runny nose. Is this normal?

Children when they first come into a setting do tend to have many colds because they are exposed to more viruses. Sleep, diet and stress can affect the immune system, so think about how settled the child is and whether they are looking tired. You should also consider whether your setting is sufficiently ventilated, especially when the heating is on, as viruses love damp warm conditions. If you have concerns, you could suggest to the parent that they talk to their GP. Do keep an eye out for signs of any hearing loss as glue ear is more common when children have colds.

Meal times

We know that food is important for two year olds' health and development. It is not unusual, though, for some two year olds to become fussy eaters, and many parents report that this can be a difficult year. We also know that there is increasing concern about the numbers of young children who are overweight, meaning food is definitely a hot topic.

Routines

Many two year olds are slow eaters. This has to be factored in when planning routines. They should be encouraged to eat and drink sitting down as this is an important habit for later on. Look out for chairs that are comfortable for children to sit in and check that the height of chairs allows children to put both feet flat on the floor when sitting. This is not just more comfortable for children, but also gives them more stability. Look out also for cups, plates and cutlery that will allow children to be as independent as possible.

Teaching the skills

At two years, you might expect children to be able to use a spoon proficiently. Their next step should be to master the use of a fork and spoon together, assuming that this is culturally appropriate. To make eating easier it is worth looking out for plates that have a rim, or putting food into a bowl to start with. When introducing a fork, think about providing foods that lend themselves to being 'speared', such as pieces of soft carrot. In terms of feeding skills, you could also show children how to push food on to the spoon using the fork and vice versa.

Getting it right

- Allow sufficient time for meals and snacks.
- Check that the tables and chairs are the right height for children.
- Observe children's feeding skills to identify next steps.
- Expect that children will sometimes play with their food.

Food and love

One of the problems when it comes to looking at food is that it is not just seen as 'fuel' for the body. Food is often an expression of love and concern. This makes it harder for adults to respond logically when a child is not interested in eating, and harder also to refuse 'treats'. Understanding that food and emotion are entwined is important because it is usually at the heart of parents' anxieties and concerns about food.

Fussy eaters

There are many reasons why children may refuse to eat all or some of their food. Whatever the reason, it is important that adults stay calm and relaxed so that the child does not associate meal or snack times with tension.

Portion size

Getting the portion sizes right for two year olds is a useful starting point. Some children appear to be fussy eaters and are refusing food because they are actually full! In addition, making children clear their plates when they have indicated they have eaten sufficiently can lead to problems later in life and is sometimes a cause of overeating. A good practical guide that looks at portion sizes for two year olds is 'Eat Better, Start Better: Voluntary Food and Drink Guidelines for Early Years Settings in England' and can be found on the Children's Food Trust website, www. childrensfoodtrust.org.uk. It is useful because not only does it give a breakdown of the types of foods, it also has photographs that clearly show how much food should be on the plate.

This nursery makes sure that breakfast and other meals are healthy

Changes in appetite

It is normal for both adults and two year olds to have fluctuating appetites. A child who may be hungry one day, may not be so the next. Instead of focusing on how much a child has eaten during a single meal, the key is to consider how much and what a child has eaten over a week.

Tiredness

As with other aspects of children's development, tiredness can have a huge impact on children's ability to cope with new food and also on their appetite. Making sure that children are not over-tired before meal times is therefore essential.

Tips for happy meal times

Pick and mix

There is some research to show that we are programmed to eat more when food is varied and colourful. A good strategy to support both healthy eating and also to avoid fussy eating is to provide a variety of different textures and colours, e.g. several types of vegetable rather than one.

Involve children

Children seem to enjoy snack and meal times more when they can be involved. Consider looking for ways to involve them in setting up the table, but also in helping themselves to the food. Many children like dipping foods in sauces and so providing little bowls of sauce can help children to experiment with new foods or vegetables that they have not tried before.

Be flexible

It is useful to be flexible in your approach to meal times. Stress is to be avoided at all costs as otherwise children will associate meal times with unhappiness. It is important not to overreact if a child is not interested in one particular food, as individual nutrients can be found in a range of foods. This means that, if a child dislikes green beans, we just need to find a substitute, such as peas.

For children who have got into a negative pattern with their food, think about having the odd picnic and being relaxed about the order in which food is eaten. In order to take this flexible approach it is essential that all food served to children is healthy and nutritious.

Avoid focusing on puddings

Traditionally, there has been a lot of focus on puddings, with children being urged to finish up their main course so that they can get their pudding. Many dieticians believe that this approach is not helpful. The underlying message that it gives children is that the 'meal' is something that is not very nice and so therefore a reward has to be given. It also teaches children that sweet is better than savoury. While puddings can be offered, they have to be nutritionally as good for children as the main course and should be low/no sugar. Fruit and dairy-based foods are considered to be better than cakes, for example.

Attractive

There is an old adage that 'we eat with our eyes' and this seems to borne out by the way that children are attracted not just to colourful foods but also to foods that are presented well. There are many ways of doing this:

- Using plates and cups that children find interesting or fun.
- Cutting food into shapes, e.g. circles of bread, using cutters.
- Creating patterns with foods, e.g. a slice of tomato between some peas.
- Creating pictures with foods, e.g. placing carrot sticks in mashed potato to make a hedgehog.

Role modelling

Two year olds seem to be more inclined to eat when they see others eat, including adults. If you work in a mixed-age group, you might sometimes like to put older children on to a table with younger ones – providing of course that they will be positive role models. Children also pick up adults' attitudes to food. If they do not see us eating green vegetables, but instead see us eating crisps or biscuits, they are less likely to try to eat their greens.

Ideally, you should always try to eat the same food as what you are serving to children, even if your portion size is very small.

What should I do if a child has not eaten much but says that they have finished?

Assuming that you have gently encouraged the child, the best thing to do is not to make a fuss. Take the plate away. If there is a pudding, this should be offered to the child as, assuming it is nutritious, it will give the child an extra opportunity to gain some nutrients. Natural yoghurt with a banana, for example, contains calcium, potassium, carbohydrate, protein and fat.

We have a parent who is worried because their child doesn't eat any green vegetables.

Many green vegetables have a slightly bitter taste and it takes time for children to get used to this. Children who have been given a lot of fruit or sweet food can find it harder to adjust to the taste of vegetables, and this is one reason why flavoured drinks and sweet puddings should be avoided. If this is the case, the first step is to look at the child's existing diet and reduce the sweeter flavours. Alongside this, try serving a range of vegetables rather than just one and think about presenting them in different ways, including with dips at snack time, for example.

Drinking

The only drinks that are recommended for two year olds are water and milk. While orange juice may seem healthy, it needs to be watered down and strictly limited. This is because it is highly acidic and so can damage children's teeth. Other drinks, even if they are labelled as sugar free, should also be given only occasionally as they can prevent children developing a liking for water.

Children need to develop a taste for water

How much water?

There has been quite a lot of hype about dehydration in children, but this is a bit of a myth; children's brains send out a 'thirst' signal well before dehydration sets in. The only time that children need to be actively encouraged to drink is when it is hot, when the body is not as effective at sending out 'thirst' signals. Equally, there is no 'magic' amount of water that children need to drink each day. A lot depends on how active they are and also how much fluid there is in their meals. A child who has eaten cereal with milk for breakfast may be less thirsty than a child who has been given toast. It is, however, good practice, and currently a regulatory requirement, that water should always be available for children.

Getting it right

- Remind children to drink after they have engaged in vigorous physical activity or when the weather is particularly hot.

Toilet training

Most children will move out of nappies between the ages of two and three years. For some children this is a fairly relaxed transition, but for others and their parents it can be quite stressful. It is therefore worth working closely with parents and providing information about toilet training where necessary.

Readiness

One of the most important things for parents and adults working with children to know is that there is not a 'set' time when all children will be out of nappies. When children are not ready, any toilet training is usually doomed either to immediate failure or is likely to be a protracted affair. On the other hand, when adults are able to make a correct judgement about a child's readiness, children can be clean and dry within a week.

Maturity of the bladder

For children to be ready to toilet train, their bladder has to be sufficiently mature. For successful toilet training the bladder needs to release urine in a 'flood' rather than little by little. To check whether children have this maturity, look out for how long a child remains 'dry' at a time, with children likely to be ready once they can retain urine for at least an hour, although preferably longer.

Awareness of passing urine and faeces

Children also need to learn when they are passing urine or faeces. This is often obvious as children may take themselves off to a corner or may stop dead in their tracks. It is helpful in the run up to toilet training to use agreed language with children so that children start to link the sensation with the words, e.g. 'Shona, I think that your wee is coming out. Does it feel wet?' As some nappies are super-absorbent, it can be worth putting less-absorbent nappies on children so that they can feel the wetness. If this is agreed with parents, it is important to change the children's nappies promptly to avoid nappy rash. A prompt change should also be accompanied with the explanation of 'getting clean'.

Getting used to the potty or toilet

Some children are able to pass urine when they hear the sound of running water. It is therefore useful at home for parents to encourage their child to sit on the potty or toilet while running the shower or bath. While this is a reflex, it can help the child to feel the sensation of passing urine and also to feel confident about using the potty/toilet. Similarly, some children pass faeces at regular times in the day and encouraging the child to sit down at those points can also be helpful.

Motivation

Children also have to be interested and motivated in toilet training. This is sometimes a harder one to crack. In mixed-age settings, younger children are often keen to keep up with older ones, and so this is sometimes a good motivator. Having some attractive underwear can also help, as can letting children choose a potty. It is important, though, however motivated a child is, that you are sure they are physically ready, as if children have repeated accidents they may lose their confidence. Equally, it seems important not to delay the move out of nappies once children are physically ready and aware.

Getting it right

- Make sure that parents know the signs of toilet readiness so that they can look out for them at home.
- Avoid trying toilet training before you are sure that children are physically ready.
- Agree with parents on key terms to describe bodily functions and use consistently.
- Help children to learn the link between the sensation of passing urine/faeces and the language.
- Promptly change children after they have passed urine/faeces so that they learn to 'feel clean'.

Should we use pull ups?

People have very different views about these. While not strictly necessary, many parents and practitioners find them a useful halfway house, although some people report that children simply use them as nappies. There is little point in using pull ups unless the child is physically ready for toilet training.

Starting out

A no-fuss approach is often best once it is decided that a child is ready to be out of nappies. Simply put children in a pair of pants or pull ups, and tell them that today they may like to use the potty. Make sure that any clothes that they are wearing are easy for them to remove. Show them where the potty is. Leave them to play, but look out for signs that they need the potty rather than giving them constant reminders (see Avoiding constant reminders, below). If the child is showing signs of needing the potty, say something such as 'I think that your wee may want to come out soon, so you may need to sit on the potty.'

Avoiding constant reminders

There are many disadvantages to constantly reminding children that they should use the potty. Successful potty training requires that children themselves recognise the sensations linked to having a full bladder. If they are told to sit on the potty before their bladder is full they miss out on this learning. This means that some children become reliant on adults telling them to go the toilet. The other danger of constant reminders is that sometimes children may not actually need the potty and so become frustrated when they do not produce anything. The odd reminder after a period of time and especially if a child is showing signs is helpful, but it is worth avoiding constant reminders.

Avoiding pressure

While it is important to offer encouragement, it is essential to avoid a situation where children become so stressed that it affects their ability to release urine or faeces. There are a number of ways that we can, often unwittingly, put pressure on children. Some can be seen on the following diagram.

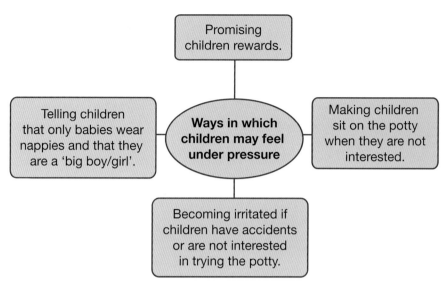

Ways in which children may feel under pressure

Promising children rewards

It may seem ironic, but promising a child a big reward may not work because the child may want the reward so badly that they are not able to relax. Quiet praise is often a better approach.

Making children sit on the potty when they are not interested

Children can become 'potty phobic' if they are made to sit down when they are not ready or interested. They can quickly associate the potty with something that they do not like.

Becoming irritated if children have accidents or are not interested in trying the potty

It is essential that all the adults involved are very realistic and open to the idea that children might need to be 'put back' in nappies.

Telling children only babies wear nappies and they are a 'big boy' or 'big girl'

While at first some children might like the idea that they are a 'big boy' or 'big girl', if they experience any failure this can make them worry that they will have to go back into nappies.

We have a child who clearly needs the toilet and becomes distressed but refuses to sit on the potty or toilet unless a nappy is put back on.

This is not unusual and often happens when a child has lost confidence or is under too much pressure. There is more than one option to consider with parents:

- Put the child back into nappies and try again after a month or so.
- See if the child will sit back on the potty while wearing the nappy, and over time progressively loosen the nappy.
- Leave out a nappy by the potty so the child has a choice of which to use.

Can a toilet be used instead of a potty?

There are no rules but there are a couple of advantages to starting with the potty. Firstly, it is possible to put it very close to the child and so some last minute accidents can be avoided. A potty also puts the child in the squat position, which in theory should make it easier for them to pass faeces. If a toilet is used, it is advisable to use a training seat. This allows the child to feel stable. It can be worth mixing and matching toilet/potty use, e.g. encouraging the child to use the toilet at home before a bath or shower, but at other times using the potty.

Handling accidents

Accidents are pretty inevitable during the first day or so. A supply of the child's own pants and clothes is worth getting from parents, as some children are put off because they have to wear someone else's clothes. It is important that accidents are dealt with in a matter-of-fact way and that where possible children are able to take some responsibility, e.g. putting on clean clothes themselves. It is also helpful to tell children that many children have the odd accident when they first start out.

How many accidents before we should give up toilet training?

While a couple of accidents on the first and second day are pretty usual, if a child has more 'misses' than hits over a number of days, it is likely that they are not ready. In some ways it is worth looking at the circumstances of the accident. A child who was on the way to the toilet or potty but just didn't get there in time is in a different league to a child who stands still and looks surprised when urine starts to appear! The latter is clearly not ready!

We have a child whose parent has asked that we remind him to go every fifteen minutes, as this is what they do at home.

I would be inclined to talk to parents about the importance of children learning for themselves the signs that they need to go to the toilet. It may also be that the child's bladder is not sufficiently mature if he needs to go to the toilet so often. If he is very thirsty and seems to be constantly drinking a lot, you should also consider whether there may be an underlying medical issue such as diabetes.

Why do some children who were toilet trained keep having accidents?

There are many reasons for this. Firstly, it is not uncommon for some children once they are out of nappies to start to lose concentration as they play or become engaged in activities. It is also worth considering whether a child has a urinary infection, as this can occur after children have been potty trained. Stress or changes at home or in the setting can also play their part, with many children regressing when they are tired or have had an emotional challenge. Finally, we should also consider the possibility, however slight, that a child might be subject to abuse, although one might expect to see other indicators.

Sleep

Most two year olds are likely to need a nap during the day. As we saw in Part 1, lack of sleep can affect children's behaviour and mean they are more likely to struggle and have more tantrums and other age-related behaviours. In addition, sleep is crucial to other aspects of children's health and well-being and is needed by children's developing immune system to ward off infections. It is linked to brain development, the processing and storage of information, so children who are not sleeping sufficiently are likely to make less progress in their learning. Interestingly, as sleep is needed for hormonal regulation, there appears to be a link between lack of sleep and obesity in childhood.

How many hours?

It is helpful to have a guide as to how much sleep most children between the ages of two and three need. It is impossible to give a precise guide as children's needs do vary, but most two year olds should be having somewhere between eleven and thirteen hours over a 24-hour period, including naps.

Signs that a child may be under-sleeping:

- is sleeping significantly under the number of recommended hours
- is irritable and generally unhappy
- has more tantrums than other children of similar age
- has difficulty waking in the mornings
- does not seem refreshed after sleep
- has frequent colds and other infections
- lacks concentration
- has dark circles under eyes.

Working with parents

Many parents are not aware just how important sleep is and may not be sure how much sleep their child should be having. Getting children off to sleep and then getting them to stay in their own bed is a very common problem for parents. It is therefore a good idea to provide parents with information about sleep and also to be ready to offer signposting to a health visitor or other services.

Helping children to sleep

Naps are important as they prevent two year olds from becoming over-tired. Interestingly, some children who struggle to fall asleep at night are actually over-tired and so may fight sleep. The difference that a nap can make to a child's ability to learn and generally cope can be immense. The human body seems to like a regular routine when it comes to sleep. We can help children to nap by creating an environment that allows the child's body to relax and helps the brain to switch off. Optimum conditions for this include:

- a darkened room
- a calm, still environment, i.e. one with no sudden loud noises or other children walking nearby
- something to pull over the body, e.g. a light sheet or blanket
- a comforter if required
- a mattress or similar, always in the same position

In addition, the timing of the nap is crucial. Wherever possible aim to create routines where the naps are earlier in the session and avoid late naps in the afternoon, unless this is what parents want. After an afternoon nap, it is important that children are given plenty of opportunities for physical activity, especially outdoors. This increases the likelihood that they will be ready for bed later on.

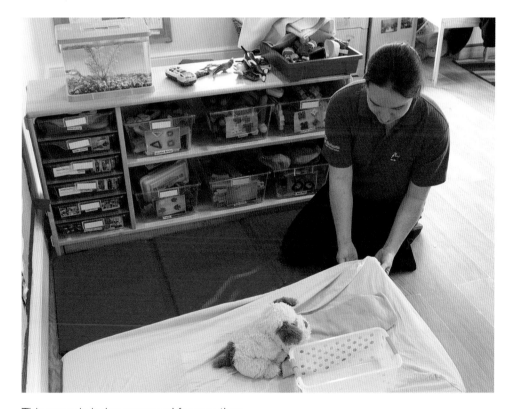

This room is being prepared for nap time

We have parents who say that we must not let their children have a nap.

As we discussed earlier, the way to approach naps is to ensure that they are taken late morning or early afternoon. Keeping a child artificially awake tends not to work because children become so tired that they drop into a deep sleep sitting at the table for tea or on the way home. Interestingly, a few years ago Ofsted, the English inspectorate, graded a setting as being inadequate because children who needed to sleep were not being allowed to. This is because children's physical well-being is thought to override parents' wishes. It can be worth developing a sleep policy so that parents know why you cannot keep children awake when it is in their best interest to nap.

We have one child who cannot sleep unless his head is stroked.

Sleep is a habit and so too is getting to sleep. Where children are used to background music, being rocked or in this case having their head stroked, they may find it hard to fall asleep without these things. Ideally, it is best to work with parents to help the child learn to fall asleep without any sleep aids. This is because during the normal sleep cycles, there will come a point where the child will awaken slightly. If their sleep aid, be it music or head stroking, is no longer available, they are likely to wake up. This is a common reason why children wake up several times in the night.

E. Creating an environment for two year olds' play

While we have focused on how best to support specific areas of children's development, it is important also to look at children's play. Play gives children opportunities to develop a range of skills and so has the potential to link to all of the areas of the EYFS and other early years curricula. Play also supports children's emotional well-being, as well as being a useful tool for learning. The importance of play for this age group is widely recognised and it is of course a requirement of the EYFS in England. Having said that, the potential of play can only be fulfilled if the right environment and resources are in place. In this section, we will look at some of the factors involved in creating an environment for play and also some common ways in which this age group plays. In Part 3, we look at adult-led activities and their importance alongside opportunities for play.

Factors to consider when planning a play environment

There are some play environments that just seem to work for two year olds. While there are no magic formulas, there are a few tips worth looking at.

Providing play at different heights

In group care settings where space is at a premium, think carefully about how many tables you need. Environments for two year olds that work well tend to have play opportunities at different heights.

Floor space

There needs to be plenty of floor space as children are likely to sit, lie and kneel on the floor as they play.

'Coffee table' height

A table or step at adult calf level seems to allow two year olds to kneel on the floor and be able to explore objects both on the floor and raised up.

Table height

If play opportunities are put at table height, expect to see children preferring to stand than sit. Standing while moving objects or exploring dough gives children better control over what they are doing.

Two year olds like being able to play with objects on top of as well as under a table

Creating spaces in group care

While a curriculum may group skills and play into areas, children are far less rigid. Having said that, in terms of planning an indoor environment, it is worth creating different spaces where children can play. Some zones may have clear play prompts, e.g. a zone that is set out with some construction materials, but others can be more flexible. There are a lot of advantages to this approach. It means you can create some spaces with specific ages/stages of children in mind. For mixed-age groups this can be a way forward where you feel the older children may need slightly different opportunities.

Organising a range of opportunities in a home setting

Ideally, you should try to create several different play opportunities within the space available. Access to books should always be available, but in consultation with the child, you may need to tidy away things before bringing new play opportunities out. Whatever your system, you should always make sure interesting resources are available that meet children's needs and interests while giving them a 'balanced diet' in terms of the early years curriculum. It is also worth thinking carefully when buying resources to make sure they will provide open-ended opportunities and be suitable for more than one age of child.

Satisfying and successful

There has to be a 'feel-good' factor for two year olds to stay engaged with an activity. It is therefore a good tip to think about the sensory impact of the resources that you put out, and about whether they will feel 'satisfying' for a child. A good example of this is the difference between throwing a fabric bean bag and a light plastic ball. One feels slightly heavy in the hand and lands with a satisfying thump, while the other is light and frankly unimpressive. In the same way, children prefer to cart around a hessian shopping bag rather than a plastic shiny one (unless of course it has a TV character on it!). This means that wherever possible you should try to choose 'real' objects over plastic toys. Also, close your eyes and think about how an action feels.

What is making this a 'satisfying and successful' experience for this child?

Children need their play, whatever it is, to make them feel successful. A beanbag landing in a metal tin might make a good sound, while marking on a white board with a dark pen allows the child to see their marks.

Observation point

- When children have found something that is engaging them, ask yourself: what is making it a 'satisfying and successful' experience?
- When a child starts but then quickly leaves an activity, think about whether it was 'satisfying and successful' for the child.

Accessing resources

There has been a lot of confusion about 'enabling environments' and what this means. Some settings have interpreted this as having everything available all of the time. While this approach does work well with older children, two year olds play very differently and often randomly tip out boxes of things. While they enjoy the sensation of the tipping, they often then move on, leaving in their wake a pretty chaotic environment. This often results in adults spending their time clearing up rather than actively and positively interacting with children. As in England the focus is increasingly on 'purposeful play', I think that it is important to evaluate carefully what and how resources should be accessed.

The best approach is probably a halfway house, whereby some resources are available, but in 'playable' quantities. This means that next to a water tray, instead of having a large box filled with resources for water play, a couple of small boxes with two or three items are put out. This still allows children to choose what to play with, but allows for more focused play. It neatly avoids situations when the water in the water tray can no longer be seen and children are therefore no longer interested. The quantity of resources can always be added to at any given time if it becomes evident that they are needed.

In the same way, a change in resources could be offered whereby children choose what they would like to get out next. In home-care settings such as child minders, this approach is fairly usual as the amount of floor space in most homes is limited and it is not possible to put out everything on offer.

Keeping play opportunities challenging

I am a great fan of the rotation of resources, especially for those two year olds who may spend 40 to 50 hours a week with us. Over-familiarity with toys and resources, no matter how good they are, often results in children losing interest (ask any parent who bought a toy on the basis that their two year old played constantly with it at a friend's house, only to find that once in their possession it was barely touched). It can therefore be useful to have a system of rotating resources and also combining resources in different ways to provide more opportunities for children.

It is likely that children who are staying for a full day will need several 'bursts' of fresh toys. The approach, of course, is to be sensible and flexible. If resources are clearly being used or are fascinating individual children or groups of children, it would be silly to say that they have to be tidied away. In the same way, having too fixed a regime, whereby at 11 a.m. everything is tidied away and new things put out, is unlikely to work as there are bound to be children who have not finished playing with the first toys.

Active play

We saw in Part 1 that two year olds are usually very active and restless. This is reflected in their play and you may also notice that some aspects of play they find 'satisfying' require gross motor movements, such as when they throw or move objects from place to place. It is therefore worth observing whether the toys and resources you provide allow for this active play.

Planning play opportunities that reflect the ways that children play

One of the key differences between two year olds and three-year-olds is the way they play. The traditional layout seen in many nurseries includes areas such as water and sand, dough, mark-making, role play and book corner. While these spaces often work well for children who are three or nearly so, I am not so convinced that they always work for children who are in their first few months of being two. It is therefore worth thinking about the ways in which many two year olds play and ensuring that the resources and activities we provide reflect them.

Play schemas

There are many theories about how and why children play, which are not explored here. Many practitioners find Chris Athey's work very helpful in identifying the features of two year olds' play. She used the term 'play schema' to identify the ways in which young children played (not just two year olds) and provided a comprehensive theory of how these link to children's cognitive development. You might therefore like to look out for her book, *Extending thought in young children: a parent–teacher partnership* (Athey, 2007).

Recognising play patterns

On a practical level, you can use play schemas or you can identify patterns in children's play to help plan your environment for children. Don't panic if you are not familiar with play schemas. Over the next few pages, we will look at a range of ways in which two year olds often play, and if you recognise these in the children that you work with, you might like to use these patterns to create play opportunities. A link has been made with the play schemas where appropriate, but do think about researching play schemas further.

Posting

Many two year olds seem to be fascinated by dropping objects into containers and either watching them reappear or having to collect them. While toys specifically for posting exist, they are often too small in scale to make playing with them a 'satisfying and successful' experience (see page 129). If the posting opportunities provided are not sufficiently engaging, you may find that children find their own at your setting. Objects may be posted down the backs of sofas in home-based settings or through the wire mesh of a fireguard! Some of the best posting containers, in my experience, are not in toy catalogues; they include kitchen bins and cardboard tubes. The action of posting is linked to the play schema 'enclosing'.

Getting it right

- Look out for a range of tubes and different recipients.
- Try to make recipients as large as possible to create more challenge.
- Try to think about the sound and feel of the smaller objects so as to provide a good sensory experience for children.
- Risk assess and supervise carefully, as many items will not have been designed for two year olds' play.

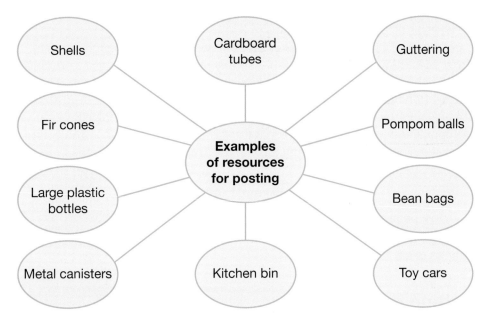

Examples of resources for posting

Providing a cardboard tube is an easy way to support posting

Dropping

As well as enjoying posting, you may also see two year olds enjoying dropping things. They may stand next to a table, simply drop a piece of a jigsaw puzzle and watch it land on the ground, before taking another piece and doing the same. Parents often report that their children at bath time will stand and drop all the bath toys into the water. This is not surprising as children tend to be fascinated by dropping things into water. Look out for storage boxes you can partially fill with water. The action of dropping links to the 'trajectory' play schema.

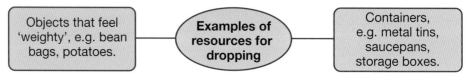

Objects that feel 'weighty', e.g. bean bags, potatoes. — **Examples of resources for dropping** — Containers, e.g. metal tins, saucepans, storage boxes.

Examples of resources for dropping

Getting it right

- If you provide water for children to drop things into, you must supervise carefully.
- Observe carefully what children choose to use for dropping, and design play opportunities based on your observations.

Open and closed, in and out

Many settings that I work with have noticed that some children are fascinated by opening and closing things. This can be the door on a toy microwave, or the curtains on a curtain pole. Instead of playing shop, they may spend time just opening and closing the cash till – much to the annoyance of older children who want to 'play properly'! In addition, you may also find that either combined with this or on its own, some children love putting things in and out of cupboards, drawers or boxes. They may spend a lot of time filling buckets up with stones or putting dolly pegs into a basket, before tipping them out and starting again. Equally they may be very happy filling up bottles with water and then pouring it out. You may also see 'in and out' when children enjoy going in and out of role-play areas, especially if a door is involved! These ways of playing are linked to the 'enclosing' play schema.

Getting it right

- Risk assess and supervise doors, cupboards and other 'openings' that may attract the interest of children.
- Look out for boxes and tins with lids.
- Organise some cupboards and drawers with which it is safe for children to play.
- Use a range of sensory materials that allow children to fill and pour.

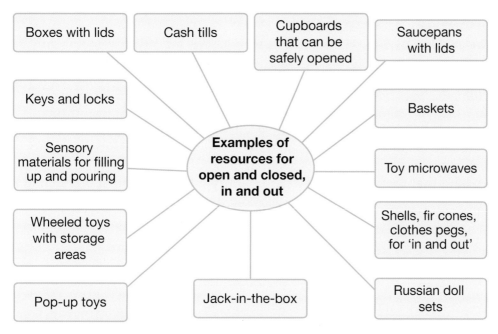

Boxes with lids	Cash tills	Cupboards that can be safely opened	Saucepans with lids
Keys and locks			Baskets
Sensory materials for filling up and pouring	**Examples of resources for open and closed, in and out**		Toy microwaves
Wheeled toys with storage areas			Shells, fir cones, clothes pegs, for 'in and out'
Pop-up toys	Jack-in-the-box		Russian doll sets

Examples of resources for open and closed, in and out

Two year olds are fascinated with things that open and close

Throwing

We saw in Part 1 that children's throwing skills are still developing, but many children love to throw. The throw usually involves picking up an object, taking it up so that it is at shoulder height, then releasing it overarm. 'Satisfying and successful' should be the mantra for providing for this type of play need. Look out for things that children can throw that are sufficiently dense that they will feel satisfying. There is, of course, a balance to be struck so that throwing can take place safely. Bean bags are helpful as they seem to be sufficiently satisfying but not so hard that there is a real danger of injury if they land on another child. In some ways, it is worth planning some throwing activities (see Adult-guided activities, page 143).

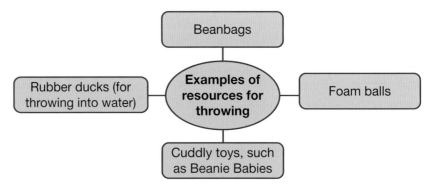

Examples of resources for throwing

Hitting and pounding

Some two year olds love the action of hitting and banging. Some enjoy making a big sound while others like the action and sensation. Think about providing sound walls outdoors where children can hit and bang a range of objects without any restriction on the noise that they make. When planning for 'hitting' you also need to be aware that some children who are not involved in this activity may find the loud noises threatening. When it comes to pounding, this can be a little quieter. You can look for items, such as a wooden pestle, that can be used to pound dough, as well as cooking activities such as mashing bananas.

Getting it right

- Think about creating a sound wall outdoors.
- Be aware that other children may not enjoy loud and sudden noises.
- Look for constructive activities that let children to hit and pound, e.g. cooking.

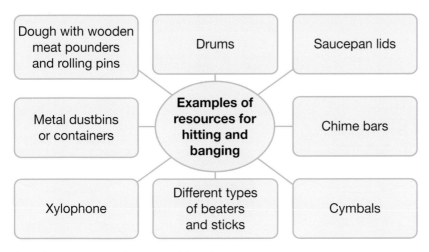

Examples of resources for hitting and banging

Transporting

'Transporting' is a brilliant term used by Chris Athey for a play schema. It sums up many two year olds' need to move things from one place to another. You can see two year olds showing this type of play on both a large and a small scale. They may fill up a bag with bits and pieces and cart it around the setting before tipping it out and starting again, or you may see two year olds who are collecting things to move around in a pushchair.

On a smaller scale, you may notice that two year olds enjoy moving a scoop of sand out of the sand tray and either dropping it on to the floor or putting into another container, if provided.

Getting it right

- Always put out sand, water or other sensory materials alongside buckets, bowls and trays so that children have a place to transport the material to.
- Look out for wheeled toys such as sit-and-ride toys and prams that allow children to put objects inside them.
- Expect that what children choose to transport may seem a little random, e.g. jigsaw puzzles, the markers from a writing table.

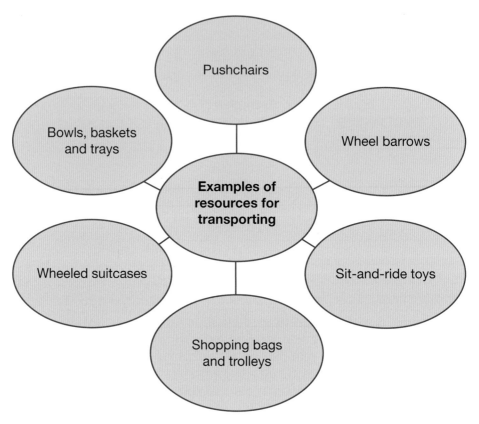

Examples of resources for transporting

Snuggling in

Many two year olds enjoy tucking themselves into the smallest of spaces. This links to the 'enclosing' play schema described by Chris Athey. You may find that large cardboard boxes that children can get inside, or even smaller ones that children can sit in, are very popular. Equally you may find that some children try to squeeze into storage boxes and baby baths. I have even seen a child try to get inside a toy washing machine! Children will also enjoy being under tables or under canopies made by stringing fabric across a corner in some fencing. The secret when trying to create snuggling-in areas is that they do need to be sufficiently small. If you as an adult can easily fit in, it is likely that they are too big!

Sometimes spaces for snuggling in can be provided by moving furniture, such as a sofa, out from a wall to create a gap. If you decide to do this, do make sure that furniture is stable and cannot fall on to the children. It is also worth remembering this play need does mean that we have to be vigilant when working with this age as children will often try to get in between the bars of railings or get stuck in narrow passages.

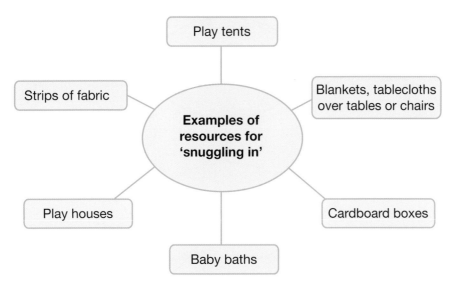

Examples of resources for 'snuggling in'

Getting it right

- Share the need for children to 'snuggle in' with parents so that they can be aware of the potential dangers in their house, e.g. wardrobes.
- Create spaces that have 'low ceilings'.
- Observe children carefully to ensure that they cannot become trapped.

Jumping and climbing

Two year olds love getting their feet off the floor. These actions link to the 'trajectory' play schema. They love steps and will even stand on wooden blocks to enjoy the experience. While some settings have good opportunities for climbing outdoors, ideally you should look at ways to allow some climbing indoors too, even if this is on a very small scale. This in a home setting might mean allowing children to climb and play on a single step, or in a group care setting finding a low stage block.

With climbing does come potential risks and so you should make sure that whatever you provide is risk assessed, especially in terms of stability. In home-care settings where children are likely to want to use chairs or sofas to climb up on, you will need to do a careful risk assessment, remembering also that even if there is little danger in your home from children jumping down from a sofa, this might not be the case in the child's own home.

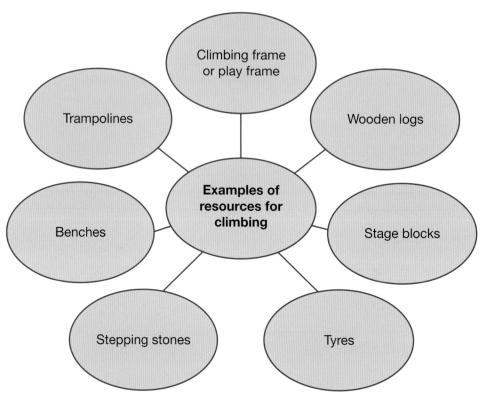

Examples of resources for climbing

Getting it right

- Risk assess climbing opportunities.
- Observe to see where children are already attempting to climb in order to make it safer.
- Provide some low climbing and jumping opportunities indoors.
- Consider developing some adult-led activities for jumping and climbing, e.g. walking on a wall.

Connecting

This is another play schema term, which describes well the way that some two year olds enjoy lining up cars, making towers of bricks or creating complex structures. Some settings report that tussles break out because one two year old has taken all the magnetic train wagons and is putting them in a line. Connecting usually requires good hand-eye coordination and so you may find it more with children who are closer to three years.

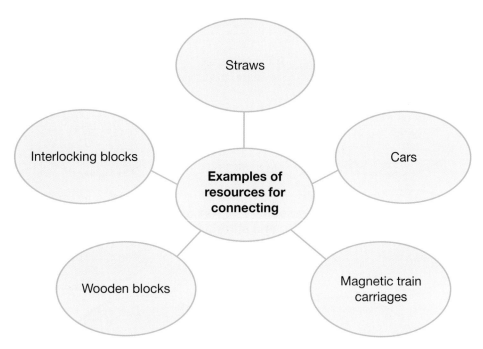

Examples of resources for connecting

Getting it right

- Observe children carefully and provide more of the same resources if you see a child engaged in connecting.
- Have additional sets of magnetic train carriages so that some can be used for just this purpose.

Mixing and stirring

Many settings find two year olds love things that they can mix and stir. They may take a paint brush and instead of painting, enjoy stirring the paint around, or if they do paint they may enjoy making a stirring motion on the paper. You may also see two year olds collecting a random selection of objects, putting them into a storage box and then enjoy mixing them up. In the same way, given a bucket of water and a stick outdoors, all manner of things will be dropped in and mixed up. Many children will also enjoy cooking activities where mixing or stirring are involved. In Chris Athey's theory, mixing is linked to the larger 'rotational' schema whereby children are fascinated by things that turn and move around.

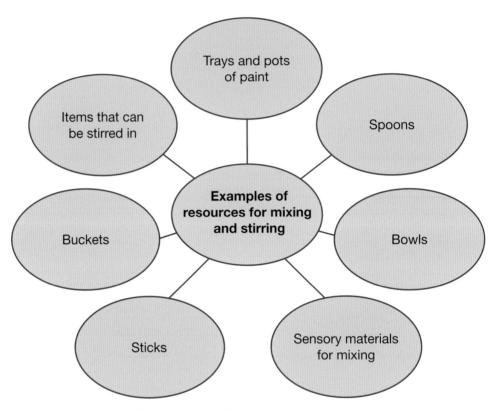

Examples of resources for mixing and stirring

Getting it right

- Expect that children will want to mix and stir materials.
- Observe to see with what children choose to mix.
- Provide trays with different colours of paint for mixing.
- Look for opportunities for cooking activities.

PART 3

Adult-guided activities

Two year olds love being busy. They also like exploring activities and new play opportunities alongside adults.

In this section we consider what makes a good adult-guided activity, as well as looking at some practical examples.

A. **The importance of adult-guided activities**

B. **Activities**

The importance of adult-guided activities

Two year olds enjoy being near 'their' adult. We have seen that even when they are happily playing alone or in parallel play, they will often just check that their adult is available. Two year olds also need times when adults are doing things with them, even if this is just a simple activity such as going to look at the fish. The best adult-guided activities are pleasurable for both child and adult. They also allow for meaningful and sensitive interactions. It is often through these interactions that children's language comes along in leaps and bounds and they learn specific skills.

Interestingly, some of the best adult-guided activities are very simple and fit closely with children's interests and stage of development. Over-complicated activities are to be avoided at all costs. They are not only unnecessary, but ironically they can actually prevent children from learning as the danger is that the adult focuses too much on the completion of the activity rather than on interacting with the child or allowing the child to explore the materials or concepts.

Tips for successful adult-guided activities

Here are a few tips that can really make a difference to whether or not an adult-led activity is successful:

Flexibility

It is essential to be flexible, as two year olds have a way of devising their own activities! A good example of this would be that while laying the table, a child might decide to pull out a chair and study the placemats. The role of the adult is then to see what is of interest to the child, which means potentially abandoning the original aim of the activity.

Quality interactions

One of the most important benefits of adult-led activities is the opportunity for children to interact with adults. Keeping the number of children down as far as possible is therefore desirable so as to ensure that children have sufficient time to interact.

Pace

Some good adult-led activities are often spoilt because adults do not adjust the pace to the children. Two year olds have their own sense of time and pace. This might mean they want to go back and look at something again, or that they lose interest and want to move on. The secret is to follow children's pace wherever possible.

Enjoyable

Adult-guided activities have to be enjoyable for children for them to have an impact. A good tip is to work from your own strengths and do activities that you personally are likely to find enjoyable. To cut down on stress, think about group size in relation to the type of activity you are doing. While blowing bubbles can be done with several children, cooking activities are much harder to do well with lots of children.

Modelling

One of the best ways of starting an adult-guided activity is by initiating the type of play or activity yourself without necessarily saying anything much to children. Most two year olds will then come alongside you and simply copy your actions. This approach is subtle and far more effective than getting children to sit down and make them watch while you give instructions.

Commentary

One of the best ways to draw children's attention to concepts such as colour, shape, size or number is simply to use a chatty commentary style, e.g. 'I love the feel of this lace.' Chatty commentaries are a natural style of interaction and seem to be more successful than using a barrage of questions.

Examples of adult-guided activities

In this following section, I have brought together a range of adult-guided activities. Nearly all of the activities can also be done outdoors, if you choose. Some will no doubt be familiar to those of you who are experienced with this age group; others build on from the common play patterns that can be seen in this age group. To help with planning and assessment, I have shown how these link to the EYFS and also more generally how they link to children's development. Many parents are interested in supporting their children's development at home; look out for the suggestions that could help learning at home, including creating displays or showing parents film clips or photographs of children engaged in an activity within your setting.

What's in the box?

Most two year olds are naturally curious. They enjoy opening things, including packets, boxes and, of course, presents. This simple activity builds on this interest and can be used time and time again. Look out for a box with a lid, such as a hat box or one that can be easily closed. Choose an object to put inside the box that you feel the child will enjoy finding. This could be a musical instrument or a shaker. Place the object in the box and put it in front of the child. Encourage the child to see what is in the box, if necessary by beginning the process of opening the box.

▲ **Safety note:** Always make sure that objects are safe for children to handle. If children are putting objects into their mouths in order to explore, take this into consideration when choosing objects.

Supporting learning at home

Provide parents with a list of simple items that they may have at home that they could use to repeat this activity, such as teaspoons or sponges. Suggest or send home boxes that they could use.

How this activity supports the prime areas of the EYFS

Personal, social and emotional development

This activity can be useful for helping children to settle in as there can be a box awaiting them each day for a while after they start at the setting.

| How confident and engaged is the child? | → | Allow time for the child to initiate opening the box and do not rush them. |

Communication and language

Children are likely to want to interact and communicate with you as they discover the hidden object.

| Does the child vocalise or seek to communicate during the activity? | → | Put in familiar objects and see if the child can say what they are. |

Physical development

This activity supports children's fine motor skills and coordination and so links to Moving and handling.

| How easily does the child open the box? | → | • Adapt if necessary to make the activity either easier or more challenging by varying the objects you use.
• Look for other types of boxes to extend fine motor movements. |

Incorporating the specific areas

 Literacy

➤ Consider putting in a book as the hidden object, especially one that is the child's favourite, and then share the book with the child.

 Mathematics

➤ Put in more than one object in the box and then count each object as the child takes it out. Put objects in that are different lengths or sizes, e.g. spoons, and use words and phrases such as 'This spoon is longer/bigger than this spoon.'

 Expressive arts and design

➤ Put in objects that are tactile or make sounds. Consider putting in objects that can be used as role-play props, e.g. a toy telephone.

ACTIVITY 2

Throw it!

Two year olds often enjoy throwing. An adult-guided activity such as this can provide safe opportunities for throwing. Find some bean bags or other items that can be thrown and will feel good when thrown. Put out three different-coloured containers, e.g. a red storage box, a blue tray and a white baby bath. Pass the child the bean bag and say 'Can you throw it into the white baby bath?' Afterwards you can see if the child can retrieve an object from a named container. Don't worry if children adapt this game. They may wish to walk with the objects and drop them in or move them back and forth from one container to another.

▲ **Safety note:** Set this activity up using objects that are safe for throwing and will not hurt other children if they go astray.

Supporting learning at home

Talk to parents about how throwing is a typical activity for this age range and its benefits. Suggest that they may like to go to outdoor spaces such as parks to allow their child to throw.

How this activity supports the prime areas of the EYFS

Personal, social and emotional development
- This activity can work to build a bond between key person and child.
- Throwing can help children to release their emotions and so help them to manage their feelings.

| Does the child make eye contact with you and seem to enjoy this activity? | → | Repeat this type of activity if it seems to strengthen the key person–child bond. |

Communication and language

This activity helps develop children's listening skills. You can use this activity to draw children's attention to colours and also the names of types of container. You may also find that children repeat back to you the name of the colour or the container.

| Does the child understand words such as 'large bucket' or 'green box'? | → | • Help the child by pointing at the container as you speak.
• Allow time for the child to process information. |

Physical development

This activity encourages hand–eye coordination through practising aiming, as well as encouraging children to be active.

| How easily does the child manage to aim and throw? | → | Change the size of the containers or their grouping. |

Incorporating the specific areas

Literacy	➤ Consider taking photographs of this activity to create a simple book with the children and write some captions underneath, such as 'Aran threw the ball into the blue bucket.'
Mathematics	➤ Count the number of objects in each container afterwards. ➤ Choose objects of different sizes and shapes and talk about these.

Animals in the tube

Many two year olds love posting. They need opportunities to practise turn-taking with an adult leading the way, and also opportunities to learn the name of objects. In this simple activity, children will be able to build on these skills. Look out for a tube into which a cuddly toy will easily fit. Put out a basket with a range of different cuddly toy animals inside. Model how you can drop an animal into the tube. Ask each child to choose an animal to drop into the tube. When the tube is full, encourage the child to lift it up and watch the animals tumble out. Expect that some children may want to hold on to an animal rather than post it.

▲ **Safety note:** Make sure that all cuddly toys are clean and safe to use.

Supporting learning at home

Talk to parents about children's fascination with posting. Collect together cardboard tubes so that parents can take one home to repeat this activity with their child.

How this activity supports the prime areas of the EYFS

Personal, social and emotional development

- This activity can help children practise turn-taking and cooperation
- This activity supports children's self-esteem as they will be making choices about which animal to put in.

- Do the children enjoy this activity?
- Do the children make eye contact with each other?

→

- Repeat this type of posting activity with other cuddly toys.
- Show children that you appreciate their cooperation by saying how well they played together.

Communication and language

This activity helps children's listening and understanding. You could also ask children to find a particular animal or size of toy, e.g. 'Can you find a small one?' Try also to create a language routine by using the same phrase over and over again as they drop in the animals. This may encourage them to repeat it, e.g. 'Down it goes!' or 'Shall we look now?'

Do children show understanding when you give them an instruction?

→

Either simplify instructions or, if children show good understanding, add in additional words, e.g. 'Can you find a *small* animal?'

Physical development

This activity encourages hand–eye coordination as children have to post the animal.

How easily do children manage to post the cuddly animals?

→

Use different lengths and diameters of tubes.

Incorporating the specific areas

Literacy	➤ Look out for books that have animals as a theme, e.g. *Dear Zoo* (Campbell, 2010).
Mathematics	➤ Put out some animals that are too big for the tube to provide an awareness of size and shape. ➤ Count how many cuddly animals fit into the tube.

Washing day

Two year olds love water. They also like helping adults. This activity builds on both of these while also helping to develop children's communication and physical skills. Look out for two buckets, one with slightly soapy water and the other for rinsing. Put out a laundry basket with some small clothes or rags to be washed. Ask one or two children to help you. Model how to wash the clothes, rinse them and then wring them before hanging them up.

▲ **Safety note:** Use cool water and do not leave children unsupervised near water. Check with parents first in case children have a skin condition or allergy.

Supporting learning at home

Show parents film clips or photographs of their child engaged in this activity but ensure that you have the parents' written permission for filming prior to this. Suggest some activities children could do at home, such as washing or wiping the shower or bath with a sponge while supervised.

How this activity supports the prime areas of the EYFS

Personal, social and emotional development

This is good for helping children to enjoy being with an adult and/or another child. It also helps children to feel that they are taking some responsibility.

Do children show signs of enjoying each other's company? ➤ Look for other adult-led activities where children can be involved in pairs.

Communication and language

This is a great chatting activity. Allow plenty of time for children to think and respond to your comments. Expand on what children say.

Do children talk about what they are doing or repeat what you say? ➤ Acknowledge children's communications by repeating what they have said using slightly longer sentences.

Physical development

Washing and wringing out clothes and rags strengthens children's hands. Passing pegs to you to hang up the clothes will also help hand–eye coordination and help strengthen hand preference.

Do children manage to wring out the clothes and rags? ➤ Look out for other opportunities to strengthen hand movements, such as play with sponges and water.

Incorporating the specific areas

 Mathematics
➤ Talk to children about the sizes of clothes or the lengths of rags.
➤ Count as you hang the items on the line.

 Expressive arts and design
➤ Make up a wash day song with the children or sing 'Rub-a-dub-dub'.

Bringing in the washing

We know that two year olds are active and restless. They also like opportunities to help adults. This simple activity for one or two children builds on this and follows on from Activity 4. In this activity, the children will help you bring in the washing. Put out a laundry basket and also a separate box or basket for the pegs. Place these some distance away from where the washing is hanging. This is because children like to move between one place and another. Unpeg the washing and give one child a peg to put in the peg box and give the other child the now dried clothing to put in the laundry basket. Encourage the children by showing that they are doing well, although do expect that they may later on sit in the laundry basket or tip out the box of pegs and play with them!

▲ **Safety note:** Make sure that the washing line is too high for children to reach so cannot cause a strangling hazard.

Supporting learning at home

Explain to parents the importance of children helping at home as a way of stimulating language, but also to keep two year olds active. You could show them photographs of this activity.

How this activity supports the prime areas of the EYFS

Personal, social and emotional development

This activity can help children practise turn-taking and cooperation. It also supports children's self-esteem as they feel they are being trusted.

- Do the children enjoy this activity?
- Do the children make eye contact with each other?

→

- Repeat this type of 'helping' activity.
- Use eye contact as well as words to acknowledge children's help.

Communication and language

This activity helps children's listening and understanding. You can talk about the colours of items as well as what they are. You can also talk about size and use expressions such as 'here's another one', that children may echo back.

Do children repeat the name of the item or show understanding when you direct them?

→

Use a similar phrase each time you give a child an item, e.g. 'Here's another peg!'

Physical development

This activity encourages children to think about things being clean and so links to health and self-care. It also encourages movement and coordination.

How easily do children manage to take items to the correct baskets?

→

Model the folding of the clothes so that they can eventually develop this skill.

Incorporating the specific areas

	Literacy	➤ Look out for books that have washing as a theme, e.g. *Washing Line* (Walker, 2007).
	Mathematics	➤ Count how many items are left on the line when there are only a few. ➤ Sometimes give children two pegs or two items of clothing and encourage them to count them.
	Understanding the world	➤ Look out for photographs showing people from around the world involved in washing.

Teddy in the bag

Two year olds are curious and they also like finding things. For this activity, look out for a fabric bag with a Velcro, zip or button fastening. Put a teddy bear in the bag along with two or three other items, e.g. a cup and a teaspoon. Show the bag to the child and let the child open it. Allow the child sufficient time to explore the objects and talk to the child about what has been found. Expect that some children will ignore the teddy and instead focus only on the objects, or that they may then go off to incorporate the objects as part of their play. If you wish to do this activity with more than one child, make sure that they have a bag each to avoid disputes.

▲ **Safety note:** Choose objects that are clean, robust and do not pose a choking hazard. If you use a drawstring bag, make sure that the cord when pulled is no longer than 25 centimetres.

Supporting learning at home

Talk to parents about grouping toys and objects together to support play at home. Explain that different combinations are more likely to engage children for longer.

How this activity supports the prime areas of the EYFS

Personal, social and emotional development	This activity can help children to settle in if you do it every day at the start of the session. It also supports children's confidence as they learn to explore new things.

How confident is the child to look inside the bag and explore new objects? →	• If children are not confident, repeat using the same objects. • For children who enjoy this activity, look out for more unusual objects, such as a dragonfruit or Russian dolls.

Communication and language	• This activity may encourage children to talk as they want to share with you what they have found. • You can name objects accurately and use positional language, such as 'inside' and 'outside'.

Do children try to communicate with you? →	Look out for objects that will be a surprise for the child to find and so will encourage them to talk.

Physical development	The bags used for this activity can encourage children to practise the movements needed for dressing, e.g. buttons, Velcro and zips.

How easily do children manage to open the bag? →	• Provide bags that have different openings to support dressing skills. • Look out for Velcro openings for children who find this difficult.

Incorporating the specific areas

Understanding the world	➤ Look out for objects that will remind children of their homes and communities.
Expressive arts and design	➤ Choose objects that have different textures and allow time for children to decide how to play with them.

157

ACTIVITY 7

Going to the library

As well as playing outdoors, children need opportunities to learn about their surroundings. A trip to the library is ideal for this. Start by finding out where the local library is and making contact with a librarian. You may find that the librarian will offer a library card for your setting or will set aside some time to guide you through the best books for two year olds.

You will also need written parental permission before the outing. During the outing, take photographs of children at different points in their journey. Allow enough time for stopping and starting and also for children to enjoy looking at the books in the library.

▲ **Safety note:** Walk the route and visit the library beforehand in order to carry out a risk assessment.

Supporting learning at home

Bring information back for parents about the library services. Invite parents to join you next time you visit the library.

How this activity supports the prime areas of the EYFS

Personal, social and emotional development

- This outing helps children learn how to meet new people and be in a new environment.
- This activity supports children's confidence as they choose books.

How confident is the child in the environment and with meeting a new person?	➤	• Allow children time before pushing them to say hello to someone new. • Prepare children for other outings by showing them photos of where they will be going.

Communication and language

As well as chatting and pointing out things to children during the visit, use photographs of the outing to help children reflect afterwards on what they have done.

Do children draw your attention to things of interest to them during the outing?	➤	Respond to children's interest and consider taking some photographs as well.

Physical development

This activity helps children to be active, but handling the books also helps children's fine motor development.

How easily do children manage the walk?	➤	Look for other outings to build up children's walking stamina, but remember that they do need a 'stop–start' approach (see Large motor movements and coordination, page 102).

Incorporating the specific areas

 Literacy

➤ Going to the library can promote children's interest in books. Listening to a story and handling books helps children become familiar with books.

 Understanding the world

➤ Talk to children about what libraries do and encourage children to point out landmarks or things of interest on the journey to the library.

Laying the table

Before a snack or a meal time, one or two children can help to lay the table. This is a good activity to do with new children, as the simple routine will help them to build a relationship with their key person. It is also a good 'chatting' activity as children are often relaxed when they do something regularly. Encourage children to put out placemats and then to pass you cutlery, which you can name. You can also create placemats that are like templates to show children where the plate, cup and cutlery go.

▲ **Safety note:** Keep an eye out for children climbing up on to the table, and supervise the handling of cutlery.

Supporting learning at home

Talk to parents about how helping with everyday tasks, such as laying the table or putting out breakfast items, can support children's development.

How this activity supports the prime areas of the EYFS

Personal, social and emotional development

This simple activity helps children to spend time with an adult and also gives them a new skill, which will help them to gain in confidence.

| How confident do children seem with this activity? | → | Look for other opportunities for children to do everyday tasks, such as sweeping the floor or wiping the table. |

Communication and language

- This activity helps children to learn words linked to meal times and can also help them to follow instructions.
- Check that children know the names of the objects used in laying the table, such as knife, fork, placemat, etc.

| Do children seem to recognise or say the names of the objects used to lay a table? | → | Repeat this activity so that children start to become familiar with the words associated with meal times. |

Physical development

- Laying a table encourages children's hand–eye coordination and helps to strengthen children's hand preference.
- Talk to children about the food that they most enjoy as part of the Health and self-care aspect.

| How easily do children manage to hold cutlery? | → | Look for other two-handed activities where children use a stabilising hand and an active hand (see Handedness, page 51). |

Incorporating the specific areas

Mathematics	➤ Count out the number of places with children before you lay the table. ➤ If you use a placemat template so that children know where to put things (see above), they will also be matching shapes.
Understanding the world	➤ Take a photograph of the children eating. Put up a display of photographs showing, for example, birthday meals or wedding meals that show different types of meals.

ACTIVITY
9

Fridge magnets

Many two year olds are fascinated by fridge magnets. They enjoy putting them on to fridge doors or other metal surfaces and then pulling them off. For this activity, collect together a wide range of fridge magnets, including those sold as gifts and souvenirs. Look out for a safe metal surface where this activity can be carried out. With the fridge magnets in a metal tin or bowl, show the child how they can be put on to the metal surface. Let the child play with the magnets and chat about magnets that seem to interest them. Don't worry if the child seems more interested in the way that magnets 'stick' to each other or to the sides of the tin. You may also find that some children are interested in lining up magnets.

▲ **Safety note:** Risk assess fridge magnets to check for potential choking hazards and to check the magnet is completely secured to its backing.

Supporting learning at home

Talk to parents about how playing with magnets helps children to practise sorting and counting.

How this activity supports the prime areas of the EYFS

Personal, social and emotional development

- As some magnets may not always stay on the surface, children will also have to persevere and manage any frustration.
- Children may gain a sense of achievement when they manage to manipulate the magnets.

How do children cope when magnets fall off the fridge or do not behave as the child expected? → Acknowledge children's frustrations sympathetically.

Communication and language

- This activity is likely to prompt children to communicate with you. They may show you what they have found in the tin and how it stays on the metal surface.
- Talk to children about the images on the magnets.

Do children try to draw your attention to what they are doing? → Acknowledge children's communications and also look out for magnets that will be of interest to children.

Physical development

This activity supports children's fine motor skills and hand–eye coordination.

Do children manage to manipulate the magnets so that they will stay on the fridge? → Look for magnets of different shapes and sizes so that children's hands make different movements.

Incorporating the specific areas

Literacy	➤ Look for magnets that have some words on them. Read the words to the children to increase their vocabulary.
Mathematics	➤ Count as the child puts the magnets on the fridge. ➤ Talk about the different shapes and sizes. Encourage the child to sort them.

Rolling objects

We have seen that children love posting things down tubes. They also like watching things roll. For this activity you will need either a long cardboard tube or a piece of guttering. Collect together in a basket or a box a range of objects that will all roll. This could include cars, pompom balls or even oranges. Holding the tube or guttering, model how things roll down. Let children take turns to find objects and then watch them roll down. Don't worry if they do not always retrieve the objects afterwards. You can tidy up together when there are no more things to roll!

▲ **Safety note:** Put tubes or guttering away afterwards to prevent children from swinging them around!

Supporting learning at home

Show parents a film clip or photographs of this activity. Talk to them about how this and other posting or dropping activities can be used to help children count items.

How this activity supports the prime areas of the EYFS

Personal, social and emotional development

As the adult is involved by holding the tube or guttering, children learn at first hand the importance of cooperation and the skills of playing with someone else.

| Does the child enjoy playing with you? | → | Show pleasure at playing with the child. Ask if they would like to hold the tube or guttering so that you can drop an item down. |

Communication and language

If you repeat a phrase each time an object is dropped, such as 'There it goes,' children are likely to try and copy it. This activity also helps children to follow simple instructions.

| Does the child repeat words or try to communicate with you during the activity? | → | Repeat this activity another day using the same phrase and see if children seem to remember it. |

Physical development

This activity is good for hand–eye coordination but also keeps children active as they stand to roll or to retrieve the rolled object.

| Do children manage to lift the object and place it accurately in the tube or guttering? | → | Look out for other activities that require children to put objects in others with some precision. |

Incorporating the specific areas

 Mathematics

➤ Choose objects that are different weights as well as sizes. Count the number of objects that are left to roll. You could also include some objects that are too big to fit down the tube or guttering.

 Understanding the world

➤ This activity links to the aspect 'the world'. Talk to children about objects with which they are familiar that might roll, e.g. toy cars, footballs and oranges.

Base camp

Two year olds love small spaces and traditionally tend to hide under tables and behind sofas. This activity can be done in and out of doors. Drape a tablecloth or piece of fabric over a table and keep it in place using tablecloth clips. Take a teddy, a bowl and a spoon and place these inside the base camp or den that you have now constructed. Encourage the child to enter into their new 'home'. Once they are inside, pass them additional items with which to furnish their base camp, such as a cushion, a blanket or even a toy mobile phone. Peer in from time to time to see how they are doing. Be ready for children to spend time going in and out of their base camp and expect that they might want to collect toys and other items to take inside it.

▲ **Safety note:** Check that objects are safe, as children will be partially out of sight.

Supporting learning at home

Suggest that parent recreate this activity with children at home. Also, let parents know that self-directed talk helps children to practise talking but that too much background noise can prevent it.

How this activity supports the prime areas of the EYFS

Personal, social and emotional development

This activity can help children to feel secure and so to manage their feelings. This type of play opportunity can sometimes encourage children to play together, but do expect that a few tussles might occur.

| Does the child enjoy being in their base camp? | ➔ | Create other small spaces where children can safely hide away. |

Communication and language

Talk to the child while you are building the base camp. Take your lead from the child as to whether or not they wish to talk. Take some photographs that can be used to prompt communication later on.

| Does the child talk to him/herself? Does the child attempt to communicate with you? | ➔ | Use this as an opportunity to record children's self-directed speech. |

Physical development

This activity helps develop children's fine motor skills, and also helps their self-care skills as they are likely to pretend to do everyday tasks, such as feeding teddy.

| Do children practise self-care skills with teddy? | ➔ | Use teddy to encourage children to practise other self-care skills, such as dressing. |

Incorporating the specific areas

Understanding the world	➤ This activity links to the aspect 'people and communities'. Take a photograph of the base camp and put it alongside other photographs of types of homes, including tents and houses.
Expressive arts and design	➤ This activity links to the aspect 'being imaginative', as children use the props to create their own ideas for play. Encourage children to help you build the base camp by providing them with choices of fabric and objects that can be put inside.

Bubbles

There is something about bubbles that all children love. Two year olds enjoy catching bubbles as well as trying to blow them. Look out for different bubble products, including those that blow tiny bubbles such as the ones used for weddings and celebrations. Talk to children about the size of bubbles being blown. Help children to blow their own by holding the container of liquid for them. This is also a great activity for two year olds to play together, with an adult leading the way, and also for mixed-age groups to come together.

▲ **Safety note:** Check with parents that children are not allergic to bubble mixture and supervise carefully to prevent the bubble mixture from going in their eyes.

Supporting learning at home

Talk to parents about how bubbles make an inexpensive play opportunity as well as encouraging and aiding children's spatial awareness.

How this activity supports the prime areas of the EYFS

Personal, social and emotional development

This activity can help children to gain confidence as they blow and catch bubbles. It can also help them manage their feelings.

Do children become frustrated if they cannot manage to blow a bubble? ➤ Provide children with a little more support and acknowledge children's disappointment.

Communication and language

Model how to blow bubbles as well as providing instructions. Use similar phrases every time they catch a bubble to encourage speech, e.g. 'Got it!'

Does the child try to communicate with you during this activity? ➤ Take some photos of this activity so that you and the children can look at them together.

Physical development

Bubble blowing and catching improves hand–eye coordination. It also helps children's spatial awareness.

Can children catch large bubbles easily? ➤ Repeat this activity and see if children can catch smaller bubbles.

Incorporating the specific areas

Literacy	➤ Follow this activity up with the book *Bubble Trouble* (Mahy, 2013). Encourage children to point to pictures of bubbles.
Understanding the world	➤ Encourage children to explore what happens when bubbles are blown outdoors on a windy day. See what happens if bubbles are blown through a funnel or straw.

Dustpan and brush

The simplest activities that adults take for granted are fascinating for two year olds. One of these is using a dustpan and brush. Take out a dustpan and brush and invite a child to help. If more children are interested, it is worth getting additional sets. As two year olds are more interested when they are using 'proper' equipment,

do not bother with toy equivalents. Sweeping up is a skill and so expect to model this and also be aware that children may not be very efficient at it! Don't worry if some children deliberately drop bits on the floor to sweep up. It's just a sign of enjoyment!

▲ **Safety note:** Keep an eye out for sharp edges if metal dustpans are used.

Supporting learning at home

Make a display with photographs showing the importance of children helping with domestic tasks, and encourage parents to try this activity at home.

How this activity supports the prime areas of the EYFS

Personal, social and emotional development

This activity gives children time with an adult, either individually or in pairs, which helps to build relationships.

| Do children enjoy this activity? | ➤ | Show children that you enjoy their company. Aim to create other similar routines. |

Communication and language

Children can learn words associated with sweeping. Try to repeat simple phrases, such as 'another sweep' or 'nearly there'.

| Does the child start to repeat some of the words or phrases that you use? | ➤ | Acknowledge children's vocalisations and repeat words or phrases back to them. |

Physical development

- Using a dustpan and brush helps children's hand preference as they are required to use each hand for a different function.
- Talk to children about keeping things clean as part of the Health and self-care aspect.

| How easily does the child manage to manoeuvre the brush? | ➤ | Try to make this a daily activity. |

Incorporating the specific areas

| **Understanding the world** | ➤ Collect together different types of brushes for children to explore, including make-up brushes, brooms and scrubbing brushes. If possible, display photographs from around the world of people using brushes. |
| **Expressive arts and design** | ➤ Leave out a dustpan and brush outdoors or in a 'base camp' so that children can incorporate these items into their play (see Activity 11, page 166). |

Shoes and bags

Children love trying on shoes – the fancier the better! They also like handbags of all sizes and shapes. For this activity, collect together a range of shoes and handbags. Look out for ones that are glitzy, such as sequinned evening bags or shoes that are brightly coloured. Put them in a basket or box. Model sorting through the shoes and bags to get children interested. Start putting the shoes into pairs and talk about matching them up. Point to features of shoes, such as 'heel' and 'buckle', so that children develop the vocabulary. Expect that children will wander off with the shoes or put them into the bags rather than sorting them. This is all part and parcel of this activity and will lead nicely on to Activity 15.

▲ **Safety note:** To avoid accidents, do not put out high-heeled shoes.

Supporting learning at home

Talk to parents about how playing with shoes and bags will prompt children to communicate. Also suggest that parents sometimes hide objects such as keys or notebooks in a bag for children to find.

How this activity supports the prime areas of the EYFS

Personal, social and emotional development	This activity supports children's self-concept and confidence as they can pretend to be older.

> **Do children enjoy this activity?** ➤ Look out for other opportunities for children to take on 'grown up' roles, e.g. cooking, cleaning.

Communication and language	• This activity helps children to learn vocabulary relating to shoes and bags. Name the types of shoes or bags accurately. • Children may also talk to themselves (self-directed speech), which helps them to practise their language.

> **Do children start to recognise the names of any of the types of shoes or bags?** ➤ Look out for other activities that will help children to learn words relating to everyday objects, e.g. clothes.

Physical development	This activity helps children with their self-care skills as they put on shoes and open bags.

> **How easily do children manage to put on the shoes or explore the bags?** ➤ Look out for shoes and bags that will help children to use buckles, buttons and zips.

Incorporating the specific areas

Literacy	➤ Look out for books that involve shoes, such as *One, Two, That's My Shoe!* (Murray, 2012).
Mathematics	➤ Sort shoes into different lengths and see if children can help you. Draw children's attention to words such as 'long' and 'short', 'big' and 'small', as well as 'narrow' and 'wide'.

Sorting shoes

This activity leads on from Activity 14, but could be adapted for a range of different situations. We know that children enjoy sorting and will also enjoy tidying up if it seems fun. Begin by taking photographs of some of the shoes used in Activity 14. Put the photographs on to shoeboxes. Work with children to see if they can put the right shoes in the right boxes. This activity will help children's physical skills, but is also good for matching and learning to follow simple instructions. Don't worry if children choose to take shoes out of boxes once they have been put away. It is quite usual to find that two year olds become interested in things when they are about to become unavailable!

▲ **Safety note:** Check that the boxes will not cause paper cuts.

Supporting learning at home

Talk to parents about how tidying and sorting can support children's mathematical skills as they can talk about size and shape with their children.

How this activity supports the prime areas of the EYFS

Personal, social and emotional development	This activity helps to build children's confidence as they learn to tidy away.
How do the children respond to this activity? →	Integrate simple and quick tidying activities into everyday routines.

Communication and language	This activity helps children's listening and understanding. Ask children to find a certain type of shoe, e.g. 'trainer' or 'flip flop'. Use the photographs as visual aids. Talk also about who might wear certain shoes, e.g. baby shoes, women's shoes.
Which names of shoes do children recognise? →	Repeat this activity another time and change the type of shoes for the children to find.

Physical development	This activity requires hand–eye coordination as children have to open the shoebox and place the shoes inside. You could also see if children can stack the boxes afterwards.
How easily do children manage to put the shoes in the boxes? →	Look for other tidying opportunities involving putting objects inside boxes and stacking them.

Incorporating the specific areas

Literacy	➤ You could model writing by adding the type of shoes on to a label, e.g. 'sandal', 'trainer'.
Mathematics	➤ This activity supports mathematics through the sorting of shoes. Children can be encouraged to match shoes together into pairs. You could also put out shoes of different sizes and see if children can order them from the largest to the smallest.

ACTIVITY 16

Photo picture lotto

Two year olds love finding pictures of themselves, family members and friends, and so creating individualised picture lotto should work well. Start by sourcing nine digital photographs for each child and printing out two copies of each photograph. Take one set of photographs and attach them to a single piece of card to form the lotto board. Use the other set to create a set of playing cards. Start by letting children explore the cards before trying to introduce the game. The game requires that children take it in turns to pick up a card and see if it matches one on the board in front of them. As two year olds are still learning to play, you might like to play with only two children at a time.

▲ **Data Protection Note:** If you are using photos of children with their family, you will need explicit written permission from the parents expressing that they are happy for photographs of their child and family to be used in this way.

Supporting learning at home

Talk with parents about the value of using photographs as prompts for communication, including encouraging children to point to things of interest and encouraging them to talk about these.

176

How this activity supports the prime areas of the EYFS

Personal, social and emotional development

This activity helps build children's self-esteem, as they enjoy seeing photographs of themselves. It also helps children to learn to take turns.

> Do the children recognise themselves and their family members? ➔ Create other games and activities using photographs in this way, such as snap or Kim's Game.

Communication and language

This activity is likely to encourage children to want to communicate and talk about the photographs on the cards and board. You can also draw attention to the details on the photographs as you look at them together, e.g. 'You are wearing a red jumper in that one.'

> Do children communicate with each other during this game? ➔ Help children to listen and respond to each other and plan other similar activities accordingly.

Physical development

This activity requires hand–eye coordination in order to manipulate the cards and to place one over another. Expect, though, that children will often lift cards up from the board too!

> How easily do children manipulate the cards? ➔ Look out for other fine motor skill games, such as in Activity 19.

Incorporating the specific areas

	Literacy	➤ You could print out another set of these photographs and make a simple book out of them. Write a line about each photograph. This helps children to understand that words have meaning.
	Understanding the world	➤ This activity links to the aspect 'people and communities', as children become aware of relationships with family and friends. Children furthermore develop awareness that other children also have families and friends.

Planting

Two year olds love being with adults, especially if they feel part of an otherwise adult-only activity. This activity introduces children to simple gardening. It is best done between spring and early autumn so that children can see the results of their plantings. You will need seeds that children can easily handle, such as beans, peas or courgettes, some compost and a couple of seed trays – ideally plug trays

as then each seed can be put into a separate compartment. Carry out this activity on the floor or on a low table with one or two children. Fill the compartments with compost. Encourage the children to push one seed down into each compartment. Add a little more compost if necessary and then add water.

▲ **Safety note:** Use this as an opportunity to encourage children to wash their hands. Do not allow children to eat the seeds.

Supporting learning at home

Show parents a film clip or photographs of children engaged in this activity. Talk to parents about how well their child concentrates and if they enjoyed this activity. Offer to send home some seeds so that children can grow plants at home with their family.

How this activity supports the prime areas of the EYFS

Personal, social and emotional development

This activity helps children to manage their feelings and develop confidence in themselves as they learn a new skill with a friendly adult.

> Does the child enjoy carrying out the activity with this adult and respond to being given responsibility?

➤

> Look out for more 'grown up' tasks that children can be involved in, such as helping to sort out books and hang up coats.

Communication and language

This activity is a great opportunity for children to learn new vocabulary as they gain a new skill. Each time they pop a seed into a compartment, say a similar phrase to encourage them to join in. Draw attention to the features of the seeds too, e.g. 'That's a big one!'

> Do children understand the instructions and recognise that plants will grow afterwards?

➤

> Encourage children to watch the plants grow and draw attention to words such as 'stem' or 'leaf'.

Physical development

Activities where children have to find and grasp small objects, such as the seeds, are good for developing the pincer grasp (see Planning play opportunities, page 105). Washing hands afterwards links to self-care (see Hand washing, page 108) as children learn that hands must be washed after touching soil.

> How easily do children manage to grasp the small seeds?

➤

> Look for other activities where children have to hold fine objects.

Incorporating the specific areas

 Mathematics

➤ Count the number of seeds as you plant them. Talk about the size and shape of seeds, especially if you plant a range of different seeds.

 Understanding the world

➤ This activity links to the aspect 'the world' as children learn about how things grow. If you take photographs they will hopefully be able to see differences as the plants develop.

Banana smoothies

Simple cooking activities can be a great way for children to learn new words as well as new skills. The trick is to look for activities that are simple enough to allow children to be fairly independent. Making a banana smoothie is a good example. You will need some ripe bananas (the riper, the better), some natural yoghurt and a little apple juice to dilute the mixture. This activity is best done with one or two children at a time, with the adult cooking alongside them so that the children can copy the actions. Start by giving each child their own large plastic jug into which they can peel and mash half a banana. Once the banana has been mashed, add some thin natural yoghurt, stir it in and then finish off with some ready-bought apple juice. The mixture can be poured into a glass and drunk straightaway.

▲ **Safety note:** Check with parents first that children are not allergic to any of the proposed ingredients.

Supporting learning at home

Create a display that shows the step-by-step process by which children manage this activity. Suggest to parents that they might like to try this simple cooking activity at home using the same ingredients.

How this activity supports the prime areas of the EYFS

Personal, social and emotional development

From being able to make their own drink, children may gain feelings of competence and pride, which should help their self-confidence.

> Do the children seem proud of their achievements?

→ Take photographs of each step in the process, including children drinking the end product (see also Activity 20).

Communication and language

This activity helps children to learn some vocabulary linked to cooking and also helps them to follow simple instructions.

> Do children seem to understand the instructions and use any of the words associated with this activity?

→ Put out the masher, a jug and also a little water in cups outdoors so that children can recreate this activity in their play and practise the language associated with the activity during their role play.

Physical development

This activity encourages hand washing, but also builds strength in children's hands through the use of mashing. It also encourages hand preference and helps children to learn to pour.

> How easily do children manage to use the mashers?

→ Look for other activities where children could use mashers, including putting them out with soft dough.

Incorporating the specific areas

Mathematics	➤ Talk about 'half' a banana and 'one spoonful' of yoghurt. You can also count how many times it takes to mash the banana into a puree.	
Understanding the world	➤ This activity links to the aspect 'the world' as children will see how the food ingredients change through the cooking process and are transformed into a drink.	

Sorting and sticking treasure

Two year olds are like little magpies and love small things that are shiny or textured! For this activity, gather together a wide range of interesting bits and pieces for children to explore and pile them on a tray. This could include items such as buttons, lace, elastic, confetti, sequins and small pieces of paper. Provide small piece of card and glue so that children can stick these small objects to the card. You can use glue sticks or let the children have the added fun of using PVA glue and spreaders – they will no doubt spread the glue on to their hands! If you do, keep a damp cloth handy. Don't worry if children are not interested in sticking, the focus of the activity is sorting through their 'treasure'. However, if you sit with children and stick pieces on to your card, you may find they copy your actions.

▲ **Safety note:** This activity is only suitable for children who are not mouthing (see Mouthing, page 59). Make sure children do not place any objects in their mouth.

Supporting learning at home

Show parents a film clip or photographs of children during this activity. Use it as an opportunity to show how children concentrate for longer if they do not have the pressure of 'making something to take home'. Suggest that parents might wish to carry out this activity with their children at home.

How this activity supports the prime areas of the EYFS

Personal, social and emotional development

This activity is good for children's confidence as they are acting independently. It is also a way for children to learn to make choices and express themselves.

| Do children seem confident to explore the different textures? | → | Watch out for children who seem reluctant, and consider whether they need more support or if they find sensory experiences uncomfortable. |

Communication and language

This activity is likely to offer plenty of opportunities to draw children's attention to colours, textures and the properties of materials. Make sure to include some pieces of elastic as these seem to be particularly fascinating.

| Do children seem to be keen to show what they have found? | → | Name and describe objects accurately so that children can widen their vocabulary. |

Physical development

This activity encourages children to use plenty of fine motor skills. It is also good for hand preference if children spread the glue with a spreader.

| How do children manage with the glue and spreaders? | → | Encourage children to use their non-active hand to steady the container of glue before using it to steady the paper. |

Incorporating the specific areas

 Mathematics

➤ This activity can encourage children to make patterns and also to sort. Talk to children about the quantity of items, e.g. 'There are only a few of these stars, but plenty of green confetti.'

 Expressive arts and design

➤ This aspect allows children to explore a range of colours, textures and shapes in an open-ended way. It is important not to focus on the production of a product and simply to allow children to experiment.

ACTIVITY 20

Sequencing

Learning to sequence or put events in order is a useful skill for children to develop. This activity will work better with children whose language has developed enough to understand and create simple sentences. First, choose an activity such as making smoothies (see Activity 18) or washing hands (see Hand washing, page 108), and take three or four photos at each step. Make sure that you photograph the children who will be taking part in the second part of the activity, as children are more likely to engage if they see photos of themselves. Laminate the photos to make them robust. Show the photos to the children and see if together you can put them in order. Use language such as 'first', 'second' and 'then'. You may find that some children will take a photo over to where the activity took place.

▲ **Data protection:** Check that parents are happy for you to use photos of their children.

Supporting learning at home

Talk to parents about how sitting down with some photographs of the child can help them to hear the past tense and also to learn words specific to what is in the photograph.

How this activity supports the prime areas of the EYFS

Personal, social and emotional development

This activity helps children's self-image because the photographs show them to be competent. You can also talk to children about their expressions in the photographs, e.g. 'You look excited in that photograph.'

Do children seem interested in seeing photographs of themselves? → Look out for a range of photographs of children in situations that makes them look competent.

Communication and language

This activity should be a way of modelling the past tense for children, e.g. 'First we turn*ed* on the tap and then we us*ed* some soap.' Hearing the past tense will help children to learn to use it, but do not expect that they will do so straight away.

Do children seem keen to look at the photographs and communicate? → Allow time for children to look at the photographs and to process what you say about them.

Physical development

This activity could be a good way to help children remember self-care skills such as washing hands or dressing. It reminds children of how to do the skill and also the order in which to do its parts.

Do children seem to recognise the order of the self-care routine? → Take photographs of children doing a range of self-care skills, including putting on shoes and putting on a coat.

Incorporating the specific areas

Literacy	➤ Turn the photographs into small books with children as a further activity. Put a caption under each photograph describing what was happening.
Mathematics	➤ This activity links to the aspect 'Shape, space and measure' as you will be talking about time and what has happened. Aim to do this activity soon after the original activity (e.g. making smoothies, washing hands) has taken place.

Feet off the floor

We know that many two year olds love to be on a raised surface. We also know that balancing is an important physical skill that involves coordination. This activity starts off by identifying a range of opportunities that will allow children to walk along a raised surface. This could be a low wall, a log or a beam. Ideally, it would be great to incorporate this activity into a walk in your local area. Encourage children to walk on the raised wall, log or beam by holding their hand and walking alongside them. For children who are more confident, walk alongside them without holding their hand, but be on standby to help them jump off or get down.

▲ **Safety note:** Risk assess the stability and height of the raised surface before allowing children on it.

Supporting learning at home

Talk to parents about the importance of physical activity for children's health and well-being. In particular, large movements will eventually help children's handwriting and ability to sit still and so help them to cope with formal schooling.

How this activity supports the prime areas of the EYFS

Personal, social and emotional development

Physical activity seems to raise children's self-confidence as they learn that they can tackle things alone. You can use this activity to acknowledge children's feelings as you talk to them and find out, for example, if they might be feeling anxious or excited.

Do children seem to enjoy the challenge or were some more nervous? ➔ Look out for other physical activities that will increase children's confidence, such as going on a swing or climbing up a climbing frame.

Communication and language

If children are concentrating, you may find that they are not able to listen and talk at the same time. Most of the communication will therefore take place either before or after the activity.

How much communication takes place during the activity? ➔ Try to develop a phrase for when children reach the end of the wall or beam, such as 'One, two, three, and jump.' Use this for other activities too.

Physical development

Walking and balancing are good for children's coordination. Expect to have to steady some children if they are not used to this type of activity.

How easily do children manage to walk on the wall or beam? ➔ Look out for other activities involving walking and balancing, e.g. draw chalk lines on the ground for children to follow.

Incorporating the specific areas

 Literacy
➤ Look out for books about climbing or going up and down, such as *Up and Down* (Jeffers, 2011).

 Mathematics
➤ This activity links to the aspect 'shape, space and measure' if you use positional language with children such as 'up', 'down' and 'along'.

Hungry puppet

Two year olds usually like puppets and using them in an activity can help build children's vocabulary and help them to communicate! For this activity, first, look for a puppet that has an opening mouth. You can make a simple puppet using a sock if necessary. Happily, children do not mind if it is very basic, with just buttons sewn on for eyes. Second, take some photos of common fruit, vegetables and food such as rice. Make these into small laminated cards. Then bring in small quantities of each food. Tell the children that the puppet is very hungry. The puppet then tells the children what they would like to eat by touching one of the cards. The children's job is to find the actual food and to see if it is what the puppet wanted – although the puppet can keep changing its mind!

▲ **Safety note:** Risk assess any food you bring in for allergies and choking hazards.

Supporting learning at home

Show parents how to use a puppet and suggest that this can be a good way to have fun together while developing children's language. Organise a puppet-making workshop for parents so that they can make their own puppets using socks or wooden spoons.

How this activity supports the prime areas of the EYFS

Personal, social and emotional development

This activity can raise awareness in children that other people may like foods that they don't like. Make sure that the puppet chooses foods that you know the children do not like or that the puppet refuses food that you know the children like.

Do the children seem happy to help the puppet?

➤ Arrange other activities where a puppet or cuddly toy is involved.

Communication and language

This activity helps children to follow instructions and also learn the names of common fruits, vegetables and other foods.

Are any of the children able to name the foods by just looking at the cards?

➤ Repeat this game with children who do not seem to know the names of common foods and add in additional foods to aid their knowledge of these.

Physical development

This activity can be used to support the 'Health and self-care' aspect. Make sure that the puppet seems to love eating fruits and vegetables and remind children of this at meal and snack times.

Do children seem to be interested in the fruits and vegetables?

➤ Chop up the fruits and where necessary prepare the vegetables following the activity for the children to taste.

Incorporating the specific areas

 Literacy

➤ Look out for books about mealtimes, such as *The Tiger Who Came to Tea* (Kerr, 2006).

 Mathematics

➤ Talk to children about how many things the puppet wants to eat. Use the language of portions, such as 'spoonful' or 'cupful', and if possible cut some fruits and vegetables into halves.

Treasure box

Two year olds love surprises. They can also be very creative and enjoy putting things together. In this activity we put a few simple toys, such as cars, play people and farm animals, in a box with everyday items, such as small cardboard boxes, funnels, corks and shells. The idea is to let children explore the different resources and combinations. You can stand back a little in this activity and take an interest where necessary. While some children will focus solely on the everyday items, you may find that other children will want to push a car into a cardboard box or put a clothes peg on the leg of a dinosaur. As long as their play is safe, anything goes!

▲ **Safety note:** Risk assess all objects carefully, especially for choking hazards and sharp edges.

Supporting learning at home

Show parents a film clip or photographs illustrating how, by bringing together a mixture of toys and everyday items, children seem to concentrate and be creative.

How this activity supports the prime areas of the EYFS

Personal, social and emotional development

This is an 'I can do' type of activity. It helps children to gain confidence as they are able to choose with what to create and play.

Do the children seem happy to explore the resources without prompting? ➔ Repeat this activity regularly and acknowledge children positively as they concentrate and play.

Communication and language

Children may not say very much if they are busy, but they may at times want to show you what they are doing. It is worth filming their play and showing them clips afterwards so that you can talk about their play together.

Do children point to and talk about what they were doing when you show the film clips? ➔ Show the film clips again and stop where necessary to allow children to express their thoughts and ideas.

Physical development

This activity is good for children's fine motor development, but also for their hand–eye coordination. Aim to provide different weights and sizes of items so that children really do have a variety of movements to make.

How well do children manipulate the resources? ➔ Repeat this activity, adding to the range of resources.

Incorporating the specific areas

 Mathematics

➤ This type of activity is fantastic for supporting children's concepts of shapes and measures as they are likely to try out different ways of using the different materials and media.

 Expressive arts and design

➤ In this activity children are able to both explore and be imaginative. It is important, though, that they have enough time to develop their ideas.

Jigsaw puzzles

Jigsaw puzzles seem to support several aspects of children's development, including logic, spatial awareness and fine motor movements. This activity involves learning to do a jigsaw puzzle, and will require adult support to begin with and is an excellent adult-led activity. If children have no experience of jigsaws, start with a four-piece jigsaw so that children achieve success quickly; avoid floor puzzles, though, as these can be harder to manipulate. Show the child the picture on the box so that they are able to match the pieces. You should also encourage children to look at pieces to work out which way up they go. Acknowledge children's success as they put in each piece.

▲ **Safety note:** Use wooden puzzles if children are likely to still be mouthing.

Supporting learning at home

Talk to parents about how jigsaw puzzles can help children's logic and problem solving. Collect jigsaw puzzles that can be lent out.

How this activity supports the prime areas of the EYFS

Personal, social and emotional development

This activity helps children develop a concept known as 'delayed gratification', whereby a little patience and perseverance is required to gain success.

| Do children persevere and are they pleased with their results? | ➔ | Repeat, but select puzzles that, while providing a challenge, are developmentally right for children. |

Communication and language

This activity requires us to sensitively prompt children in order to guide them, e.g. 'We have the man's head and body, so should we look for the feet now?' Expect that children may not talk much, but will be focused on the 'doing'.

| Are children able to follow the prompts? | ➔ | Collect a range of puzzles that will act as prompts to help children learn different vocabulary, e.g. animals, parts of the body. |

Physical development

This activity helps children's fine motor skills and hand–eye coordination as they have to be quite accurate in their movements.

| How well do children manipulate the jigsaw puzzle pieces? | ➔ | Provide a range of different jigsaw puzzles, including chunky ones as well as ones with smaller pieces. |

Incorporating the specific areas

 Mathematics

➤ Jigsaw puzzles are good for children's logic and problem solving. They also help children to look at shapes carefully and so link to the aspect 'shape, space and measure'.

 Understanding the world

➤ The pictures on jigsaws can be used as a talking point to support the 'people and communities' and 'the world' aspects. Look out for jigsaw puzzles with pictures of animals or people in roles such as firefighters.

Hide and seek with teddy

While most two year olds are not good at searching, they still enjoy joining in treasure hunts. This activity, will helps children follow simple instructions and have fun. It is best done with one or two children. Start by hiding teddy in a fairly easy place for them to find – peeping out from under a cushion or sitting on a low shelf. Tell the children that teddy wants to play hide and seek and we need to look for him. Ask them where they think he might be. Look with the children, but give them huge clues as to where he is. Then see if the children want to hide and have teddy find them. If yes, put out some fabric for them to hide under, or suggest safe places where they could hide. Tell them when 'Teddy is coming' and show mock surprise when you and teddy find them.

▲ **Safety note:** Supervise children carefully, especially if they take turns to hide.

Supporting learning at home

Talk to parents about playing games with their children, such as hide and seek. Explain how this can help to develop children's spatial awareness and creativity.

How this activity supports the prime areas of the EYFS

Personal, social and emotional development
- This activity helps children to persevere, as they may not find teddy straight away.
- Children also enjoy the 'thrill' of hiding and being found.

Do children seem to enjoy finding teddy and also hiding? → Think about other games involving finding or hiding things, such as hunt the thimble or sleeping lions.

Communication and language
- This activity helps children to learn language relating to position, such as 'on top of' or 'underneath'.
- Point to teddy and say these phrases so that they can learn these words in context.

Do children seem to be able to find teddy following the clues? → Repeat the activity but introduce more words to describe where teddy is, such as 'next to the blue box'.

Physical development

This activity helps to develop children's spatial awareness as they look around them.

How easily can they find teddy? Do they have a good sense of spatial awareness? → Repeat this game, but play it outdoors on a larger scale. Choose places to hide teddy that require children to look more carefully.

Incorporating the specific areas

 Literacy
➤ Look out for books about hide and seek, such as *Hide-and-Seek Pig* (Donaldson & Scheffler, 2011).

 Expressive arts and design
➤ This activity links to the 'being imaginative' aspect as children are pretending to hide. If you put out fabrics or boxes children can also make places to hide.

Making sparkling shakers

A simple and popular activity is to make shakers. You will need some small clear plastic bottles (200 ml is a good size) and three or four funnels. Collect a range of sparkly materials, including sequins, stick-on jewels, shiny beads and sweet wrappers. Put out a range of dried materials, including rice, corn and pasta shells, in different bowls each with a scoop. Show the children how to scoop some rice and funnel it into the bottle before adding some shiny bits and pieces. Encourage children to create their own mixtures rather than dictate what should go in. When they have made their shakers, glue the lids before screwing them on the bottles and allow the glue to set firm. This activity is best done on a very low table to allow children to manage the funnel.

▲ **Safety note:** This activity needs close supervision and may not be suitable for children who are still mouthing.

Supporting learning at home

Ask if parents would like to take the shakers home and give them some ideas of how they could be used, such as turning on some music and seeing if children can shake in time to a beat or stop when the music stops.

How this activity supports the prime areas of the EYFS

Personal, social and emotional development

Activities where children make things for themselves help them to become proud of themselves. Music-making, i.e. shaking in time to music, alongside others can help children to develop relationships.

> Do children enjoy making and using the shakers? ➔ Think about other music-making activities for children, e.g. games involving music such as musical statues or musical bumps.

Communication and language

This activity will help children's listening skills. When they have made their shakers, see if you can model the vocabulary linked to the sounds they make, e.g. 'loud', 'quiet', 'soft'.

> Are children able to follow instructions once you have modelled the activity alongside them? ➔ Look out for other simple activities where children can make things, such as cooking activities or making bookmarks using marbling inks.

Physical development

This activity helps children to use tools, which will help their hand–eye coordination.

> How well are children able to use a spoon and funnel to fill the shakers? ➔ Look for other opportunities for children to use a range of tools, such as a hole puncher or a stapler (under supervision).

Incorporating the specific areas

Literacy	➤ By creating different types of shakers, children will hear the differences in sounds. This is a pre-reading skill. Encourage children to use the shakers to accompany spoken nursery rhymes, too.
Expressive arts and design	➤ By encouraging a range of choice in creating their shakers, children are able to explore and design what might be their first musical instrument. Put on some music so that they can accompany it with their shakers if they wish.

ACTIVITY
27

Wind-up toys

Many two year olds are fascinated by wind-up toys. As some can be fragile, they often require an adult to be on hand. This is an activity that works well with one or two children, or more if some of the children are older. Collect a range of wind-up toys and also musical boxes. Make sure that a few are sufficiently robust for children to operate independently as the children will want to have a turn. Try also to look for some that might light up or make a sound so that children can make the connection between turning the mechanism and the toys working. Talk about what they do and how many twists are needed for the wind-up mechanism to work. Ideally, try to open up one of the toys so that children can see how it works.

▲ **Safety note:** This activity needs close supervision and is not suitable for children who are mouthing.

Supporting learning at home

Suggest to parents that they keep an eye out for wind-up toys to use with their children, but let parents know that children may overwind the toys unless they are robust. Parents might like to look out for two wind-up cars that can be used together for races.

How this activity supports the prime areas of the EYFS

Personal, social and emotional development

This type of activity requires collaboration between the children and the adult. It also helps children to learn to take turns and to treat objects carefully.

| Do children handle the wind-up toys carefully? | ➤ | Look out for other opportunities where children can be trusted to take care of delicate items, e.g. showing children a spider's web. |

Communication and language

This activity is likely to prompt the odd squeal of excitement and also interest from children. Talk to children about what is happening and model accurate language, e.g. 'It's spinning more slowly now.'

| Are children keen to talk about what they are seeing? | ➤ | Take photographs of the wind-up toys and musical boxes so that children can request them again. |

Physical development

Turning a wind-up mechanism requires children to make a rotational movement with their hands while using a pincer grasp (see Planning play opportunities, page 105). This is a skilled hand movement.

| How easy do children find the rotational movement required to wind the mechanism? | ➤ | Provide opportunities for children to develop this movement with activities such as turning keys or using a spinning top. |

Incorporating the specific areas

 Mathematics

➤ There are opportunities to speculate about how far a wind-up toy might travel and also opportunities to group them into types, e.g. toys that work in water on one side, musical boxes on another, etc.

 Understanding the world

➤ This activity links nicely to the aspect 'technology', as children learn about gadgets and how their actions can make what is effectively a simple machine work.

Feeding the animals

Many two year olds are interested in animals. They like looking out for cats and birds, and even worms and spiders. However, they do need an adult to guide them when touching or feeding animals. For this activity, think about what opportunities there are in your setting for children to feed an animal. You may have a pet already, so involving children in the feeding could be part of your everyday routine. If your setting does not have a pet, go to a park to feed the ducks or create a bird table. You might also consider getting a fish tank, as going to watch the fish is a great way of settling children in. Chat about the type of food the animal likes and why it is important to wash hands after feeding or touching the animal. As you might expect, this activity is one where children must be closely supervised.

▲ **Safety and data protection note:** Always check with parents that children do not have allergies or phobias. Ensure children are supervised at all times when around animals. If taking photos, ensure you have written permission from parents.

Supporting learning at home

Find out if parents have pets at home and if so encourage them to use this as an opportunity for children to count (e.g. count the animals), measure (e.g. measure out animals' feed) and be responsible.

How this activity supports the prime areas of the EYFS

Personal, social and emotional development

This is an activity that develops children's sense of competence as they take on some responsibility for the care of an animal.

Do children enjoying feeding the animals? ➔ Look out for other activities that involve some responsibility, such as wiping tables after an activity or meal time, or helping an adult to lay the table (see Laying the table, page 160).

Communication and language

This activity helps children to listen and follow instructions. They can also learn words connected to the animal that you are feeding. Talk to children about the types of food that different animals eat.

Do children seem to recognise words linked to this activity? ➔ Take photographs of the activity so that children can talk about feeding the animals afterwards.

Physical development

This activity will probably require children to stay still or move slowly around some animals, as well as involving hand movements.

How easily do children control their movements, especially staying quiet and still? ➔ Look for games where children have to stay still for a few seconds, e.g. 'sleeping lions'.

Incorporating the specific areas

Literacy	➤ Link this activity to books about animals, e.g. *The Very Hungry Caterpillar* (Carle, 1969). Consider taking photographs of children putting out food for the animals and creating a book with them afterwards.
Mathematics	➤ There are plenty of opportunities for measuring and counting, e.g. 'How many scoops of food should an animal be given?' or 'How many pieces of bread will that duck eat?'

Washing salad

Simple cooking is a great way to encourage children to develop healthy tastes. This activity is a great one to do in the summer months. Bring in lettuce, tomatoes, cucumber and any other vegetable that could be made into a salad. Take children over to a sink and let them rinse each of the vegetables. Accurately name the items children are washing. Talk to children about why we wash fruit and vegetables. If you have a salad spinner, let children see if they can make it turn. Otherwise, use kitchen towels and encourage the children to dry the vegetables. Afterwards, see if they would like to taste any of the vegetables.

▲ **Safety note:** Check with parents first that their children do not have any food allergies.

Supporting learning at home

Show parents photographs of their child involved in the washing activity so they can see that this is a possible activity to do at home.

How this activity supports the prime areas of the EYFS

Personal, social and emotional development

Cooking activities, especially this one involving water, are likely to be popular with children. They give children confidence and help them to learn to take turns.

> Do children enjoy this activity and are they able to be cooperative? ➔ Look out for other activities where children can be involved in a task together.

Communication and language

This activity gives children the chance to chat to you as they wash the vegetables and also to learn the names of the items they are washing. It is therefore an activity that involves listening and understanding.

> Do children enjoy following the instructions? ➔ Remember to give only one instruction at a time and if necessary to model it.

Physical development

This activity links to Health and self-care as you encourage children to try vegetables that they may not otherwise have tried. It also helps children to learn about the importance of washing and keeping things clean.

> Are children ready to try any of the vegetables? ➔ Look for other cooking opportunities using fruit or vegetables, such as making fruit salad or soup.

Incorporating the specific areas

Literacy	➤ Take photographs of this activity and make it into a book. Write a caption under each photograph so that children can see how prints link to the spoken word.	
Understanding the world	➤ If children go shopping with you for some of the vegetables, they will make the link between the local environment and this activity. You can also link this to foods that they eat or don't eat at home.	

Bottles and lids

Two year olds love playing with water. They are also interested in opening and closing things. In this activity, we combine these two play interests. Look out for a large container suitable for putting water in – this could be a storage box, a baby bath or the conventional water tray. Put out a range of different bottles – all with their lids in a basket or box nearby. Play alongside children, modelling how to push the bottle down to allow it to fill, then putting the lid on. You could put out a couple of sponges and model how to use them to fill the bottles. You could also model pouring water from one bottle to another. This is definitely an 'aprons on' and sleeves-rolled-up type of activity.

▲ **Safety note:** Never leave children unattended around water, and change the water regularly to prevent the spread of infection. Also ensure that you use only plastic bottles (not glass).

Supporting learning at home

Talk to parents about the benefits of water play and suggest simple activities that they could try at home, e.g. providing a bucket of water, a teaspoon and a bottle – children will spend a long time filling the bottle by spooning water into it.

How this activity supports the prime areas of the EYFS

Personal, social and emotional development	Play with water seems to help children to express their feelings and generally seems to hold their attention. Learning to screw and unscrew lids also gives children a sense of achievement.
How well do children concentrate during this activity? ➤	Look out for other opportunities for water play, such as dropping rubber ducks into a bucket of water or putting out short lengths of tubing and funnels for children to explore.
Communication and language	This activity can help children learn vocabulary, such as 'full', 'empty', 'open' and 'closed'. Expect that children may not chat while they are busy but may want your attention at times, e.g. when they have finished unscrewing a lid.
Do children seem to recognise words associated with this activity? ➤	Repeat this activity but use different containers so as to increase their vocabulary.
Physical development	Unscrewing bottles requires a rotational hand movement that will be a challenge for some children. In addition, putting on lids and filling bottles is useful for hand–eye coordination.
How easily do children manage to unscrew the lids of the bottles? ➤	Present water at meal times in small bottles so that children learn to unscrew the bottle and pour the water.

Incorporating the specific areas

Mathematics	➤ Look out for different sizes of bottles and present them by lining them up in order of height before the activity starts. You could also take off the lids from the bottles and see if children can work out which lid goes on which bottle.
Expressive arts and design	➤ Exploring the medium of water and its properties links closely to the aspect 'Exploring and using media and materials'. Think also about adding colour to the water.

Useful resources

Foundation Phase, Wales, **http://wales.gov.uk/topics/educationandskills/earlyyearshome/foundation_phase/?lang=en**

Curriculum For Excellence, Scotland, **www.educationscotland.gov.uk/earlyyears/curriculum**

Areas of Learning at Foundation Stage, Northern Ireland, **www.nicurriculum.org.uk/foundation_stage/areas_of_learning**

Alborough, J., 2007, *Washing Line*, Walker Books

Athey, C., 2007, *Extending Thought in Young Children: A parent–teacher partnership*, 2nd ed., SAGE Publications

Campbell, R., 2010, *Dear Zoo,* Macmillan Children's Books

Carle, E., 2002, *The Very Hungry Caterpillar*, Puffin

Department for Education, 2012, *A know how guide: the EYFS progress check at age two*, Department for Education

Department for Education, 2013, *Early years outcomes*, Department for Education

Donaldson, J. & Scheffler, A., 2011, *Tales From Acorn Wood: Hide & Seek Pig*, Macmillan Children's Books

Field, F., 2010, *The foundation years: preventing poor children becoming poor adults*, Cabinet Office

Jeffers, O., 2011, *Up and Down*, HarperCollins Children's Books

Kerr, J., 2006, *The Tiger Who Came to Tea*, HarperCollins Children's Books

Mahy, M. & Dunbar, P., 2013, *Bubble Trouble*, Houghton Mifflin Harcourt

Murray, A., 2011, *One Two That's My Shoe!*, Orchard Books

Sheridan, M., Sharma, A. & Cockerill, H., 2007, *From Birth to Five Years*, Routledge

Tickell, C., 2010, *Review of the Early Years Foundation Stage*, Department for Education

Index

abuse 16
active play 131
activity, level of 23–4
additional support 2
    adult-guided activities 144–205
importance of 144–5
adults *see* key worker; parents
adult-to-child ratios 98
age-related development 2–3
    see also development; milestones
ambidexterity 51
    see also hand preference
animals 200–1
assessment 2–4, 7–9
    see also progress check; observation
Athey, Chris 132
attachment 11–16
    factors affecting 14–16
    proximity 12–13
    separation anxiety 12, 83
    wariness of strangers 13–14
attention
    undivided 96
    for unwanted behaviour 31
babies, premature 16
background noise 95, 166
balancing 186–7
ball play 47–9
banana smoothie 180–1
base camp 166–7
behaviour 22–34, 93–4
    activity level 23–4
    attention-seeking 31
    biting 30–4
    emotions 24–5
    frustration 94
    impulsivity 22–3
    and language 23, 24, 26
    managing 28–9, 93–4
    in mixed-age settings 70
    sharing 23, 29–30
    tantrums 25–9

    see also personal, social and emotional development
biting 30–4
block play 140–1
books
    access to 128
    choosing 100
bottles and lids 204–5
breakthrough moments 5
bubbles 168–9
buttons 107
catching *see* throwing and catching
child abuse 16
choking hazards 70
circle time 35, 69
climbing 46, 139–40
coats 107–08
comforters 93
commentary 145
communication and language development 35–43
    correcting speech 97
    environment for 95–8
    and key person 77
    listening and attention 35–6
    speaking 38–42
    understanding 36–8
    see also language
communicating with parents 72, 86
    see also working with parents
confidence *see* self-confidence
conflict, avoiding 94
connecting play schema 140
consent 6
cooking activities 180–1, 202–3
cooperative play 17–18
correcting speech 98
data protection 176
dehydration 118
delays in development 8–9, 61–4
den building 166–7
depression, in parents 15